PRAISE FOR THE PLAYS OF ADAM RAPP

RED LIGHT WINTER

"Complex and compelling . . . What at first glance appeared to be a study of friendship turns, by degrees, into an exploration of passion and the perverse . . . [Rapp] has a generous talent. In *Red Light Winter*, he brings memorable news about the heart, telling us both how it fools itself and how it kills itself." —JOHN LAHR, *The New Yorker*

"An arresting study in melancholic triangulation and obsessions dashed . . . Shrewd about the way certain male friendships exist on the knife edge of disaster." —MICHAEL PHILLIPS, *Chicago Tribune*

"A tight two-act portrait of toxic male rivalry, sexual obsession and treacherous memory . . . This intense character study will amuse, arouse, shock and devastate you . . . A wildly engrossing tale of violent desire, from a passionate writer making good on his early promise." —DAVID COTE, *Time Out New York*

"A frank, graphic story of erotic fixation and the havoc it can wreak on sensitive souls, it marks a step forward for Mr. Rapp . . . here exploring a wider range of human emotion and writing with a new sensitivity to match his natural gift for crackling, hyperarticulate dialogue." —CHARLES ISHERWOOD, *The New York Times*

STONE COLD DEAD SERIOUS

"Rapp is very gifted, and, even rarer, he has something to say . . . *Stone Cold Dead Serious* [is] brave, compassionate, and at times . . . breathtakingly moving." —BRUCE WEBER, *The New York Times*

"Sharp and disquieting . . . Beneath the scurrilous comic banter and absurd surfaces is a mysterious recurrence of objects, actions, persona and language, in an oblique and haunting style reminiscent of Haruki Murakami's best fiction." —ED PARK, *The Village Voice*

"[A] scabrous, poignant vision of suburban-American innocence lost." —CAROLYN CLAY, *Boston Phoenix*

"Will leave your mind buzzing and your heart aching."
—BRANDON WOLCOTT, *Show Business*

FASTER

"Talented and highly prolific . . . Rapp . . . is brave and facile in his language, and he ventures where few writers are able or willing to go." —BRUCE WEBER, *The New York Times*

"There's no want of energy [in] *Faster* . . . [Rapp] has a rising reputation for creating fast-talking, hard-hitting characters who make up in colorful language and intensity what they lack in, well, social graces." —JEREMY GERARD, *New York*

"[Rapp] has made a name for himself writing about the darker things . . . *Faster* is no exception as it examines the complex relationship between hope and reality, faith and circumstance."
—RANEE JABER, *Show Business*

FINER NOBLE GASES

"Rapp boldly and honestly exposes a segment of society that most of us, thankfully, know only from a distance. [*Finer Noble Gases*] is a resounding warning about what happens when parents disconnect from their children and the young turn to drugs, television and other substances as emotional pacifiers."

—JUDITH EGERTON, *The Courier-Journal* (Louisville)

"These aren't your typical alienated hipsters. Mr. Rapp is aiming for something much more grand and metaphysical than just another mundane tale of arrested development."

—JASON ZINOMAN, *The New York Times*

"Rockers Chase . . . and Staples . . . are a present-day Vladimir and Estragon—hoboes with nowhere to go, waiting indefinitely for someone to rescue them . . . [and] given Rapp's view of slacker-dom as a kind of installation art, [the play] helps turn what feels like nothing into something of hypnotic beauty."

—DAVID NG, *The Village Voice*

NOCTURNE

"A startling, unnerving work of art that fiercely pushes the boundaries of theater . . . Rapp is an original—a distinctive voice . . . *Nocturne* will haunt you for a long time."

—MICHAEL KUCHWARA, Associated Press

"A brilliant, terrifying, perceptive, occasionally funny play . . . Bold, daring and successful." —DONALD LYONS, *New York Post*

"Adam Rapp's *Nocturne* is remarkable enough to bear comparisons with Margaret Edson's award-winning *Wit* . . . Here [is] a playwright . . . to watch with keen interest."

—MARKLAND TAYLOR, *Variety*

STEVEN FREEMAN

ADAM RAPP

ESSENTIAL SELF-DEFENSE

ADAM RAPP has been the recipient of the Herbert and Patricia Brodkin Scholarship; two Lincoln Center Le Comte du Nouy awards; a fellowship to the Camargo Foundation in Cassis, France; two Princess Grace awards for playwriting; a Roger L. Stevens Award from the Kennedy Center Fund for New American Plays; a Suite Residency with Mabou Mines; the Helen Merrill Award for Emerging Playwrights; Boston's Elliot Norton Award; and a Lucille Lortel Playwright's Fellowship. He was short-listed for the William Saroyan International Prize for Writing for *Nocturne*, and he received a Joseph Jefferson Award in Chicago for Best New Play, received a special citation from the Obies, and was a finalist for the Pulitzer Prize for Drama for *Red Light Winter*.

His plays include *Ghosts in the Cottonwoods* (Victory Gardens; The Arcola, London); *Animals and Plants* (American Repertory Theatre); *Blackbird* (The Bush, London; Pittsburgh City Theatre; Off-Broadway at Edge Theater); *Nocturne* (A.R.T., Off-Broadway at New York Theatre Workshop); *Stone Cold Dead Serious* (A.R.T., Off-Broadway at Edge Theater); *Finer Noble Gases* (26th Annual Humana Festival of New American Plays, Off-Broadway at Rattlestick); *Faster* (Off-Broadway at Rattlestick); *Trueblinka* (Off-Broadway at the Maverick Theater); *Dreams of the Salthorse* (Encore, San Francisco); *Red Light Winter* (Steppenwolf; Off-Broadway at the Barrow Street Theater); and *Gompers* (Pittsburgh City Theatre; The Arcola, London).

Trade editions of his plays, all available from Faber and Faber, include *Nocturne, Stone Cold Dead Serious and Other Plays*, and *Red Light Winter*.

He is the writer and director of two feature films: *Winter Passing*, starring Ed Harris, Will Ferrell, and Zooey Deschanel, which premiered at the 2005 Toronto International Film Festival; and *Blackbird*.

He is the author of six novels for young adults: *Missing the Piano* (Viking/HarperCollins); *The Buffalo Tree* (Front Street/HarperCollins); *The Copper Elephant* (Front Street/HarperCollins); *Little Chicago* (Front Street/HarperCollins); *33 Snowfish* (Candlewick Press); and *Under the Wolf, Under the Dog* (Candlewick Press), which was a finalist for the Los Angeles Times Book Prize. He is also the author of the adult novel *The Year of Endless Sorrows* (Farrar, Straus and Giroux).

Currently he is at work on a graphic novel, *Decelerate Blue*, forthcoming from First Second.

A graduate of Clarke College in Dubuque, Iowa, Mr. Rapp also completed a two-year playwriting fellowship at Juilliard. He lives in New York City.

OTHER WORKS BY ADAM RAPP available from Faber and Faber/Farrar, Straus and Giroux

Nocturne

Stone Cold Dead Serious and Other Plays

Red Light Winter

The Year of Endless Sorrows

ESSENTIAL
SELF-DEFENSE

ESSENTIAL

SELF-DEFENSE

A PLAY BY **ADAM RAPP**

FARRAR, STRAUS AND GIROUX

NEW YORK

Farrar, Strauss & Giroux
18 West 18th Street, New York 10011

Printed in the United States of America
First edition, 2007

Library of Congress Catologing-in-Publication Data
Rapp, Adam.
  Essential self-defense : a play / by Adam Rapp. —1st ed.
    p. cm.
  ISBN-13: 978-0-86547-968-5 (pbk. : alk. paper)
  ISBN-10: 0-86547-968-2 (pbk. : alk. paper)
  I. Title.

  PS3568.A6278E87 2007
  813'.54—dc22
                                          2006021488
  P1

Designed by Gretchen Achilles

www.fsgbooks.com

FOR PAUL SPARKS

ACKNOWLEDGMENTS

The author would like to thank Tim Sanford at Playwrights Horizons, David Korins and Carolyn Cantor of Edge Theater Company, and John Buzzetti at The Gersh Agency.

FEAR AND LONELINESS

Essential Self-Defense started out as a lark. An ex-roommate was telling me how she had been in a women's self-defense class in New York, in which she had to assault an attack dummy that was an actual man dressed in an enormous foam suit. My first question to her was, What does this man do? She told me that he simply stood there until he was put down. My second question was, Who would take a job like this? I imagined the late Andy Kaufman in some oversized Nerf costume. Theatrically, the image of a man wearing such a thing, being assaulted by a woman who intends to take him down, seemed like a great idea to jump-start a play. So that's what I began with. I had no idea *why* this was an intriguing possibility for an evening of theatre or where the thing might go, but it certainly felt like a man and a woman literally colliding in a women's self-defense studio was fertile soil. I also was pretty sure that some version of love would be involved, as well as notions of irrational fear, personal safety, loneliness, a scurrying sewer rat, and whatever that thing is that lurks in the woods behind the 7-Eleven.

I started thinking a lot about the play while I was at the Pittsburgh City Theatre, in rehearsals for my play *Gompers* (when I'm not directing, I'm a terrible daydreamer). I was originally going to conceive *ESD* as a two-person karaoke opera, with two locations: a self-defense studio, represented by a wrestling mat, and a karaoke bar, represented by a drum kit, a microphone and mic stand, and a cocktail table. Simplicity was heavy on my mind after watching director Tracy Brigden and the City Theatre Company production staff attempt to figure out how to make the ten-character, six-location monster that was *Gompers* work. With *ESD*, structurally, my original intention was that scenes alternate sequentially be-tween the women's self-defense studio and the karaoke bar. My characters (who even early on were called Yul and Sadie) would sing the story of their lives to each other during the karaoke scenes and then Sadie would beat on Yul in the self-defense studio, with a third character acting only as a drummer. This drummer would percussively accompany the beatings during the self-defense studio scenes, conveniently oblivious to that world, and play along with all the karaoke performances as the bar's house drummer. I thought he might also evolve into some sort of antagonist to Yul and Sadie's relationship.

When I began actually writing the play, I was bewildered by our country's obsession with the manhunt for Osama bin Laden and the blind, at-all-costs attitude to not only finding him but bringing him to a swift and certain terminal justice. It was Keystone Kops going after Big Foot, my junior high swim team diving for the Loch Ness monster. It just seemed absurd that the notion of finding this one man would somehow solve all of our problems relating to the September 11th tragedy and all of its concomitant cultural dam-age. I was also fascinated by how the media was seemingly in ca-hoots with the Bush administration in spinning a modern Big Bad Wolf myth. Every time I turned on the television I saw images of Bin Laden lurking in some Middle Eastern cave. I was also struck by the strange, almost peaceful kindness that seemed to emanate from his eyes. And then the day came when I thought, What if this guy really didn't have anything to do with 9/11? What if he is sim-ply the scapegoat fashioned by the media and the various acolytes of the Oval Office to satisfy our country's knee-jerk, Old Testa-ment need for retribution? Mr. Bin Laden has obviously had many dealings with world terror—there's no doubt an acre or two of proof on the subject—but, still, this devil's advocate stance intrigued me. Yes, it was a dangerous, unpopular, perhaps even unpatriotic notion, but I couldn't shake it.

So then the world of the play started to evolve. I started thinking of it as a Big Bad Wolf fable, and I had to increase the population in order to deal with all that find-him-at-all-costs madness; I doubt even the cleverest playwright can eke out a decent manhunt with only two characters. So from there I created a community for our two heroes to live in. I thought the civic simplicity of a butcher, a barber, a librarian, and a custodian would be an interesting way to populate this place that I eventually called Bloggs—not because of the obvious Internet allusion, but because of the great baseball player, Wade Boggs, who for me represents the best of the game of baseball, our great American pastime. I basically added an L so Mr. Boggs wouldn't be offended (though not that many Hall of Fame baseball players frequent the theatre).

After 9/11, a lot of people got really scared. "Homeland Security" became a household phrase and several of my friends back in the Midwest were taking weekend "first response" workshops on what to do in case our country was attacked. In the East Village, for months people walked around wearing surgical masks, not only to avoid inhaling the Twin Towers ash that was still thickening the air but also to prevent inhaling anthrax and a myriad of other purported urban germ-warfare contaminants. I saw a neighbor in a ground-floor apartment duct-taping his windows. An actor whom I had worked with several times admitted to me that he bought a pair of gas masks from an army/navy wholesaler on Canal Street for himself and his girlfriend. Seemingly every few minutes the dopplering thunder of jets policing the heavens could be heard overhead. There was a checkpoint along Fourteenth Street where you had to present your passport or driver's license to prove that you lived in the neighborhood. Uncertainty was viral and Big Brother was most definitely watching, and wasn't he even starting to take on vague wolflike qualities? Was that a snout protruding from under that police helmet? No, that couldn't be a snout! That's a policeman! A National Guardsman! A U.S. marshal in full fatigues and spit-shined boots! That's a civil servant!

For me, Sadie represents this uncertain American, suddenly afraid to go outside, to check behind the drapes, to reach under the bed for that lost slipper. That harmless stroll in the woods was suddenly fraught with profound, paralyzing fear. Walking into a dark room, no matter how familiar, was like walking into the arms of the bogeyman. It's the fear of everything. The fear of public toilets. The fear of the post office. The fear of deodorant sticks and sanitary napkins. The fear of opening a letter from your mother. Of gym bags left on park benches. The fear of the air we breathe. Whether or not anything actually happened to you personally, the fear was there. Or was it? Did you simply dream it? Or was it something conjured out of the undulating, pixelated gospel of your television? Whatever the case, the fear has become a new part of American culture. And it's inside you now, yes it is. It's right there, as certain as a rib.

And is Yul an antidote for or a catalyst of this fear? He certainly has plans—plans that involve injecting a mysterious substance into colored, hard-boiled Easter eggs. But is he the one responsible for all those kids who are disappearing from the local junior high school? Is this strange, sensitive loner who was recently fired from his job for drawing an "X" over President Bush's face in the daily newspaper a real threat to the community, or is he the invisible hero? Is he Bloggs's Timothy McVeigh or Kurt Cobain? And what the hell does a guy like this do when someone actually loves him? Does something soften in his heart or does he press on until he's accomplished the mission?

What I wound up with months later turned out to be perhaps more impossible to stage than my monolithic *Gompers*, as the locations became not only the self-defense studio and the karaoke bar, but also Sadie's home, Yul's rat-infested cinder-block basement apartment, a butcher counter, a library help desk, a barbershop, a hospital room, and Norvis Woods. Plus, my cast ballooned from two to ten, so perhaps what I ultimately saw stacked neatly on my desk was a play that was impossible to produce. Oh, no, not another dead play, I feared. Dead plays are like dead children and I've amassed my share of them.

Thank god for Playwrights Horizons and Edge Theater, who agreed to do a coproduction. And thank god for Paul Sparks, who, in a certain eerie light, bears a faint resemblance to both Timothy McVeigh *and* Kurt Cobain, depending on how much you've had to drink and what room he happens to be standing in.

ADAM RAPP
June 2006

ESSENTIAL
SELF-DEFENSE

Essential Self-Defense was originally workshopped at the 2006 Cape Cod Theatre Project, Andrew Polk, artistic director. It was performed on July 6, 7, and 8 and directed by the author. The musical director was Ray Rizzo. The production stage manager was Dawn Dunlop. The cast was as follows:

YUL CARROLL	*Paul Sparks*
SADIE DAY	*Emily Cass McDonnell*
BOB BEARD	*Ray Rizzo*
KLIEG THE BUTCHER	*Michael Cullen*
TODD/UPS MAN/MALE NURSE	*Lucas Papaleus*
SORREL HAZE/ SELF-DEFENSE LEADER VOICE	*Laura Heisler*
ISAAK GLINKA	*Michael Chernus*
CHUCK	*Guy Boyd*

Essential Self-Defense had its premiere in New York City on March 15, 2007, in a coproduction by Playwrights Horizons and Edge Theater Company. It was directed by Carolyn Cantor; sets were designed by David Korins; costumes by Miranda Hoffman; lights by Ben Stanton; and sound by Eric Shim. The musical director was Ray Rizzo. The production stage manager was Chuck Turner. The cast was as follows:

YUL CARROLL	*Paul Sparks*
SADIE DAY	*Heather Goldenhersh*
BOB BEARD	*Ray Rizzo*

TODD/UPS MAN/MALE NURSE	*Lucas Papaleus*
ISAAK GLINKA	*Michael Chernus*
CHUCK	*Guy Boyd*

N.B.: At the time this edition went to press, the roles of Klieg the Butcher and Sorrel Haze had not yet been cast.

CHARACTERS

YUL CARROLL, thirty, a lone wolf

SADIE DAY, thirty, still possesses a childlike innocence

BOB BEARD, heavily bearded, mid-thirties, an amazing drummer

KLIEG THE BUTCHER, fiftyish but ageless somehow, a nightmare

TODD/UPS MAN/MALE NURSE, mid-twenties

SORREL HAZE/SELF-DEFENSE LEADER'S BULLHORN VOICE, thirty, a punk-rock librarian

ISAAK GLINKA, thirty, a Russian immigrant, hopeful

CHUCK, sixty, a simple barber

SETTING

BLOGGS, a town in the heartland

ACT I

SCENE 1

The Big Beat-Down Self-Defense Studio/Kiff's Karaoke

The encounter mat, which is a polyurethane rectangular wrestling mat. YUL is standing in the center, wearing a large suit of sponge. His hair is a mess and he looks as if he hasn't slept in years. He stares out at the audience. A loud industrial-sounding buzzer sounds and then SADIE, thirty and small, enters in a fury. She wears sweats, headgear, and boxing gloves. Through an unseen bullhorn we hear the incantation "Take it back! Take it back! Take it back!" over and over again. SADIE begins using a series of pugilist–slash–martial arts combinations to attack YUL, who simply stands there and takes the beating.

In Kiff's Karaoke Room, BOB BEARD, the drummer for Bob Beard and the Unholy Stones, is seated at his drum kit. Kiff's Karaoke Room is the back room of a small dive bar. There are a half dozen or so small tables and a small raised stage outfitted with a full drum kit, two electric guitar amps, two electric guitars on stands, and a few microphone stands. As soon as SADIE begins attacking YUL, BOB BEARD scores it with accompanying percussion. He is unaware of their actions and it should seem like he's simply tuning up his drums for the evening's gig.

At the Big Beat-Down Self-Defense Studio, YUL is driven to the ground and places his arms in the air submissively. The women in the studio

cheer. "Again!" the self-defense leader yells through her bullhorn. SADIE
helps YUL *up and then exits the stage. A second buzzer sounds and then*
SADIE *rushes* YUL *again, unleashing another round of punches, kicks,*
knees, etc., while BOB BEARD *accompanies her percussively and the*
women of the studio yell, "Take it back! Take it back! Take it back!"
repeatedly. Again, this goes on until YUL *is driven to the ground and*
raises his arms in submission. The studio applauds.

"Again!" the self-defense leader yells through her bullhorn. SADIE
again helps YUL *off the mat and exits the stage. The third and final*
buzzer sounds and then SADIE *rushes* YUL *again, unleashing her*
third and final round on him. "Take it back! Take it back! Take it back
forever!" the other members of the studio yell. Again, BOB BEARD
accompanies the beating on his drum set. During a final crescendo,
SADIE *accidentally knees* YUL *and he goes down, holding his face. The*
drums cease.

SADIE Oh my god.

The members of the studio continue applauding and cheering for SADIE.
From his knees, YUL *looks at his tooth pinched between his fingers, and*
then rises off the mat, flings the tooth wildly, and lurches out of the
studio.

SELF-DEFENSE LEADER'S BULLHORN VOICE Good work, Sadie.
    You conquered the meat man and took back your power.
SADIE That was his tooth.
SELF-DEFENSE LEADER'S BULLHORN VOICE It's just a tooth,
    he'll be fine.

SADIE But I hurt him.

SELF-DEFENSE LEADER'S BULLHORN VOICE You conquered the meat man, Sadie.

SADIE I didn't mean to hurt him.

SELF-DEFENSE LEADER'S BULLHORN VOICE Yes, you did.

SCENE 2

Sadie's Kitchen/Yul's Basement Apartment

SADIE *is standing very rigidly in her kitchen. It is a simple, clean, suburban kitchen. There is a table with four chairs. She is holding* YUL*'s tooth, pacing back and forth.*

In YUL*'s apartment,* YUL *is sitting at his desk with several paper towels wrapped around his waist (as if they were a regular towel), freshly showered, boiling eggs on a portable stovetop. His apartment is a crude cement and cinder-block basement. His light is off and he is mostly in silhouette so that outside of a cot, a footlocker, and the desk, the details of his living space can't be made out.*

He is listening to a news report on the radio.

MALE RADIO ANNOUNCER   In local news, as of six o'clock this evening, area seventh-grader Edith Paul has been reported as officially missing. Twelve-year-old Paul is the twelfth student from Bloggs Junior High School to mysteriously disappear in the past three weeks. Police currently have no leads.

In SADIE*'s kitchen,* SADIE *grabs her phone off the wall and dials a number that she reads from a small piece of paper.*

MALE RADIO ANNOUNCER In other news, King Kenny, the
    leader of the East Coast–based rap group King Kenny and the
    Kings Highway Kings, pleaded guilty to four counts of . . .

In YUL*'s apartment, his phone rings. He turns the radio off, stares at the
phone for a moment, hesitates, then answers it quickly. He speaks in a
low-energy, deliberate fashion.*

YUL Yes?
SADIE Is this Mr. Carroll?
YUL Who's this?
SADIE This is Sadie. Sadie Day from the Big Beat-Down
    Self-Defense Studio. I'm the one who accidentally knocked
    your tooth out today.
YUL Oh. Hello.
SADIE I acquired your phone number from the studio's help
    desk. I hope I haven't stepped over a boundary by calling you at
    home.
YUL No, it's fine.
SADIE Oh, good.

Awkward pause.

SADIE Well, anyway, Mr. Carroll, I'm calling because I wanted to
    let you know how terribly sorry I am. I had no intention of
    kneeing you in the mouth like that.
YUL Yeah, they warned me about headgear.
SADIE I also wanted you to know that I have your tooth, and I
    was wondering if I could return it to you. I imagine losing
    such a thing could be quite upsetting. Would you like it back?

YUL I guess.

SADIE *peeks through the blinds of the kitchen window, steps away from the window. She sits, then stands again.*

SADIE What's that noise in the background?
YUL I'm preparing eggs.
SADIE Oh.
YUL "Oh" what?
SADIE Just "oh."

Pause.

SADIE Well, Mr. Carroll, is tonight bad?
YUL Bad for what?
SADIE For meeting up.
YUL No, tonight's okay.
SADIE Then perhaps we could rendezvous at Kiff's?
YUL What's Kiff's?
SADIE It's a bar on Dubois Street. It's not far from the studio.
    Right next to Bob Ortega's Supertaco Machine. Do you
    know it?
YUL Yeah, I know where Bob Ortega's Supertaco Machine is.
SADIE Well, Kiff's is right next door to that. Is nine o'clock okay?
YUL I don't have a car, so it's gonna take me a little longer. Better
    make it nine-thirty.
SADIE Nine-thirty then. Great.
YUL Is there a dress code? Because I don't think I can meet you
    there if there's a dress code. I don't do codes.

SADIE I'm almost positive that there isn't a dress code. Wear
    whatever you'd like.

YUL Okay.

SADIE So I'll see you at nine-thirty.

YUL See you.

They hang up. SADIE *peeks through the blinds over the sink, draws the
curtains, then backs out of the kitchen.*

YUL *continues sitting at his desk, still in his paper towels, listening to
the eggs boil.*

SCENE 3

Kiff's Karaoke

Sitting at tables are SADIE, *who is wearing a nice blouse with a silk scarf around her neck and some smart slacks, and* KLIEG THE BUTCHER, *the most feared man in town.* KLIEG THE BUTCHER *is sitting in the corner, brooding over a pitcher of beer. He is bald and sports prolifically tattooed forearms.*

YUL *enters wearing an orange Hawaiian shirt, JCPenney Plain Pockets, and a pair of military-issue black low quarters, unshined.*

SADIE *(standing)* Mr. Carroll!
YUL Hello.
SADIE Please join me, why don't you.
YUL Sure.

He sits.

SADIE Did you take the bus?
YUL I'm not much for public transportation.
SADIE Oh. Well, how do you get around?
YUL For a while I was using this pair of custom-made Silver Streak roller skates, but one day when I was on my way to work this evil gang of kung fu Rollerbladers came out of nowhere and hit me over the head with a pair of fourteen-inch octagon nunchakus and stole my skates and flung them into an

infectious-waste incinerator. So now I pretty much walk everywhere.

SADIE That's such a horrible story.

YUL Yeah, those skates were pretty important to me.

SADIE I trust you've had better luck lately.

YUL Luck is a concept perpetuated by casino bureaucrats and the lottery establishment.

SADIE Oh. Well, how was your walk, anyway?

YUL As good as could be expected. The constant assault of barking dogs wasn't very encouraging. This German shepherd practically read me the riot act.

SADIE With all of those kids disappearing from the junior high school, I'm sure everyone's keeping Fido in watchdog mode. I think the whole town's on edge about it . . . In any event, I'm glad you made it here safely . . . This is my favorite place. The clientele is quite varied.

YUL Looks like a lot of faking-it goes on.

SADIE Faking what?

YUL The stuff that makes the machine happy.

SADIE What machine?

YUL The one that doesn't have an off switch.

Awkward pause.

SADIE Well, how are you feeling, Mr. Carroll? Are you in a lot of pain? I brought you some Aleve, just in case.

YUL Heavily advertised over-the-counter pharmaceuticals don't interest me much. And please don't call me Mr. Carroll—I'm not your science teacher. My name is Yul. It rhymes with "mule."

SADIE And "fuel."

YUL I'm not amused by word games.

SADIE Sorry.

Awkward pause.

SADIE So did you go to the dentist? Because I'd be happy to help
you pay for the damage.

YUL Don't worry, I'm not gonna sue you. I don't trust dentists,
anyway.

SADIE Oh. Why?

YUL I'm generally suspicious of anyone who plays tricks with
trademark anesthetics.

SADIE But the anesthetic's contingent to a myriad of dental
procedures.

YUL You just used the word "myriad."

SADIE Yes. I believe its primary nominative definition is quote
unquote "a large number." Its secondary nominative
definition, albeit archaic, is actually cited as "the quantity ten
thousand." I'm pretty confident that my use of the word is
correct.

YUL It's just fancy is all. Like you wear a cape or something.

SADIE A cape?

Pause.

YUL Besides, I'm not much for procedure. I feel that way about
the medical profession in general.

Awkward pause.

SADIE Well, the band should be here in a few minutes. Do you enjoy karaoke?

YUL I've never done it.

SADIE Do you like music?

YUL I used to be in a garage band.

SADIE Oh, wow. A garage band. Where did you play?

YUL In a garage.

SADIE What were you called?

YUL The Thing That Wasn't There.

SADIE The Thing That Wasn't There. That's quite interesting. Sort of paradoxical.

YUL Isn't just about everything?

SADIE Well, it depends on one's worldview.

YUL My worldview involves ominous cloud formations and lots of shattered glass.

SADIE Oh, well, I'm sorry to hear that.

YUL It's not your fault.

SADIE I know . . . I just . . . Hmmm.

Awkward pause.

SADIE So how big was your garage band?

YUL It was pretty much just me. There was one other guy for a while, too, but he got industrial poisoning and had to be sent to another part of the country to be poked and prodded.

SADIE I see. What instruments do you play?

YUL I play guitar, drums, keyboards, lap steel, sitar, bass, the cello, the glockenspiel, and the E-flat alto saxophone. And I have this three-foot length of Primoflex tubing that makes some pretty interesting noises.

SADIE Huh. Well, I'm quite impressed. You must be very
talented.

YUL Talent is a fallacy created by gym teachers and Top 40 radio
'droids.

Pause.

SADIE So how did you wind up getting the job at the Big Beat-
Down?

YUL I got fired from this place and no one else would hire me.

SADIE Oh. Where were you working before?

YUL The plant.

SADIE The Zenith plant on Old Mill Road?

YUL I'd prefer not to use the "Z" word.

SADIE Why not?

YUL Because they're evil, soul-sucking fascists and every time I
hear that word I feel like my head might twist off.

SADIE Then I'll be sure to use its pronominal modifier in the
future. What did you do at your, um, place of former
employment?

YUL I made knobs.

SADIE Why did you get fired, if you don't mind me asking?

YUL Someone saw me draw an "X" over this guy's face in the
newspaper.

SADIE So they fired you?

YUL Uh-huh.

SADIE That seems a little extreme. Who was the guy in the
newspaper?

YUL The president.

SADIE Of the television plant?

YUL No, the other one.

SADIE Of the United States.

YUL Yeah, the genius.

Pause.

SADIE I'm in book publishing. Children's books.

YUL Do you do the pictures or the words?

SADIE I actually work on both. I'm a production editor.

YUL I don't like books with pictures. Pictures lie mostly.

SADIE Well, there are books without pictures, too. Like young adult novels. And chapter books for early readers.

YUL I'd most likely be more into them.

SADIE Are you an avid reader?

YUL I've read certain manifestos by significant historical leaders. I also like car manuals and this one particular quarterly journal that deals with population statistics. Do you have any gum?

SADIE Actually I do. Would you like some?

YUL Yes, please.

She removes gum from her purse, offers him a stick.

YUL Thanks.

SADIE You're welcome.

She watches him chew for a moment, smiles.

SADIE So how were you preparing your eggs?

YUL Excuse me?

SADIE When I called. You said you were preparing eggs.

YUL I was boiling them.

SADIE Oh, I just love them hard-boiled. I know this wonderful recipe for deviled eggs.

YUL I like 'em plain.

SADIE Oh, but deviled eggs are delicious, Yul.

YUL Please don't do that.

SADIE What?

YUL Use my name at the end of a sentence. You can use it at the beginning but not at the end. It's what the drones in human resources do when they begin the termination process.

SADIE I'll keep that in mind.

YUL Yeah, I try and steer clear of corporate discourse as much as possible.

Pause.

YUL I don't eat the eggs anyway.

SADIE What do you do with them?

YUL I can't really talk about it.

SADIE Okay.

Pause.

SADIE Would you care for a drink?

YUL I don't drink alcohol.

SADIE Oh. Are you an alcoholic?

YUL I don't like the taste. Plus, it's exactly the thing they're trying to put inside you.

SADIE Who?

YUL The heart-shrinking marketing goblins and corporate warlocks.

SADIE How about something else? Something spritzy?

YUL I guess I wouldn't mind a root beer.

SADIE Great. I'll be right back.

She exits.

YUL *and* KLIEG THE BUTCHER *share a tense look.*

KLIEG THE BUTCHER Hey, you're that guy.

KLIEG THE BUTCHER *quickly produces a digital camera, takes* YUL*'s picture.*

YUL What guy?

KLIEG THE BUTCHER The guy who lives in the sewer. The rat-lovin' loner freak.

YUL I don't live in a sewer.

KLIEG THE BUTCHER Yeah, don't think you're foolin' anyone.

SADIE *returns, holding two drinks.*

SADIE They didn't have root beer, so I got you a Shirley Temple.

YUL Those are good, too.

She hands him the drink.

SADIE That's quite a shirt, by the way. Did you get it in Hawaii?

YUL I got it at T.J.Maxx.

SADIE Well, it looks very nice on you.

YUL Thanks.

SADIE You're welcome, Yul—I mean, Yul, you're welcome.

She offers her glass for a toast. They clink glasses, drink.

YUL Your hands.

SADIE What about them?

YUL They're small.

SADIE Oh. I . . . Yes.

YUL I notice things like that.

SADIE You're quite observant.

YUL When you hit me I'm always surprised.

SADIE That I hit you?

YUL By the power produced by such a small hand.

BOB BEARD *and* TODD (*Bob Beard and the Unholy Stones*) *enter and
take the stage.* BOB BEARD *has a big black beard and wears only beads
above the waist.* TODD *wears tight-fitting pants and nothing on top. He
might have pierced nipples. His hair is dyed neon green.*

SORREL HAZE, *the karaoke hostess, enters. She has punk-rock hair and
likes to take the stage. She grabs the mic while* TODD *plugs into his amp
and* BOB BEARD *checks the tension on his drumheads.*

SORREL Good evening . . . Small house tonight. I know most of
you out there. Welcome to Wingin'-it Wednesdays at Kiff's
Karaoke. Fuck yeah, man!!! Woooooo!!!

SADIE *claps. She is the only one.* TODD *does something tricky on the guitar.*

SORREL I'm Sorrel Haze and I'll be guiding you through the festivities this evening. Before we begin I have an announcement to make. I know everyone's been hearing a lot about those children who keep disappearing at Bloggs Junior High School—I think the count is officially over a dozen. It's been devastating the community for three weeks now and I just wanted to say that if you know anything—even if you have a hunch—you can leave an anonymous tip at the Bloggs Memorial Library on Summit Street. I'm one of the librarians there and we've set up a fairly user-friendly online tip box. So don't be afraid. If you know something, SPEAK THE FUCK OUT!!!
    So, back to business! Yeah! Fuck yeah, right??!!! We only have one rule here at Wingin'-it Wednesdays: No cover songs! Originals only! And you don't get out of the room unless you sing, right, Bob Beard?!

BOB BEARD *punctuates this with a flurry of drums and cymbals.*

SORREL Just sing your song, the band'll catch on faster than you can say "Suck my fuckin' BOOTS!!!" So without further ado, let's give it up for Bob Beard and the Unholy Stones!!! *(She leads an applause, while* BOB BEARD *and* TODD *execute their signature riff.)* Come on, fuckers!!!

Everyone claps, SADIE *more enthusiastically than the other two.*

SORREL Right on! So who's our lucky number one?

KLIEG THE BUTCHER *stands, cracks his knuckles.*

SORREL Klieg the Butcher! Right on, man! I like that initiative!

KLIEG THE BUTCHER *approaches the stage.*

SORREL And what are you gonna sing for us this evening?
KLIEG THE BUTCHER A song called "Klieg the Butcher's Right
    Hand Is the Strongest Human Appendage in the World, So
    Don't Even Think About Challenging Him or He Will Crush
    Your Bones."
SORREL Well, all right!!! That's a rockin' title!!! Let's give it up for
    Klieg the Butcher!!!

Everyone claps except for YUL, *who is not impressed.*

KLIEG THE BUTCHER *takes the microphone, stares out at the few
assembled, crazy with intensity, and then begins to sing a menacing song
about the pure power of meat and how infallible his right hand is.*

KLIEG THE BUTCHER *(singing)*
    In the cold war warming
    The crowd stepped aside
    To heed the calling
    Get in line

There's a black horse coming
Horses coming
Low-down for the rest of my life

Tell the children
What you've done
To Mother Earth
And the sun

There's a black horse coming
Horses coming
Cure the meat and cover your eyes
There's a black horse coming
Horses humming
And Vin Diesel's running out of lines

(breaking from the song, a heraldic,
hyperbolic truth)
BUT KLIEG THE BUTCHER'S RIGHT HAND IS THE
STRONGEST HUMAN APPENDAGE IN THE WORLD, SO
DON'T EVEN *THINK* ABOUT CHALLENGING HIM OR
HE WILL CRUSH YOUR BONES!!!

God loves you.

He crushes something impressively, like a pint glass.

SORREL *(joining him onstage)* Talk about fucking ominous. Nice
work, Klieg the Butcher. Who's next?

KLIEG *exits the stage, victorious. He sits back at his table.* SADIE *stands.*

SORREL Sadie Day. Get your pretty little ass up here.

SADIE *joins her onstage.*

SORREL What are you singing tonight, Sadie?

SADIE *(nervous)* A song about grass and squirrels.

SORREL Grass and squirrels—that's fucking awesome. Let's give
it up for Sadie! Come on, fuckers!!!

Some clapping. SADIE *clears her throat, nods to* BOB BEARD *and*
TODD. TODD *begins a sweet folk song on the guitar, ballad-like.*

SADIE *(singing)*
   The squirrels have found a way up to the mountaintop
   When they are afraid they make like they're bunnies and
      they hop
   Hop hop

   Through the grass the grass says "Go!"
   It will not tell the squirrel "No—you cannot be a bunny now.
   I'm sorry you must stop."
   Go
   Hop hop

   The mountaintop is where squirrels with black eyes can go
   High above black forests, they can see their home down below
   Low low

Through the grass the grass says "Go!"
It makes the mountaintop feel not so bad
If it's not the home it's the best place
The squirrels have known

Since they've been home.
Hop hop.

SORREL *(joining Sadie onstage)* Let's give it up for Sadie Day!

Applause.

SORREL How did that feel, Sadie?

SADIE Oh, it felt wonderful.

SORREL Excellent. It sounded wonderful, too.

SADIE Thanks, Sorrel.

SORREL You're welcome. Now who's next?

SADIE *exits the stage, sits back down at her table with* YUL. YUL *stands, approaches the stage.*

SORREL And who are you?

YUL Yul Carroll.

SORREL Well, hello there, Yul Carroll. You from Bloggs?

YUL Yes.

SORREL Havin' a good night?

YUL Not particularly.

SORREL Why not?

YUL I don't know. Getting my tooth knocked out might have
   something to do with it.

SORREL Well, I'm sorry to hear that. I hope things turn around
  for you.

YUL Me too.

SORREL So what are you gonna perform for us this evening?

YUL A song.

SORREL What's it called?

YUL Um . . . I don't know yet.

SORREL Well, that's cool. Sometimes the title reveals itself to us
  in mysterious ways, right?

YUL I guess.

SORREL Right on. So let's give it up for Yul Carroll!!!

SORREL *applauds, sets the mic on its stand, exits the stage.*

YUL *(to* TODD*)* Can I borrow your guitar?

TODD *nods, hands him the guitar.*

YUL *(singing and playing)*
  Many many many . . .
  Many nights have I slept
  In a basement the days forget

  Many many many . . .
  How many days did you go
  Through the streets all alone

Many many many . . .
Count the ways you were preapproved
Count the ways a body can be moved

Many many many . . .
How many coupons did you save
For purchases you threw away
(Can you) stand to sleep where you stay
Will it rain when they take you away

Many many many . . .
How many rounds can you last
In a game where you have
To make a present from your past
To stare at faces from a digital mask
How many checks can you cash
Before the supermarket's crashed
CRASHED CRASHED CRASHED CRASHED
MANY MANY MANY MANY MANY MANY MANY

(breaking from the song, an enormous,
terrified announcement)
AND HOW MANY TVS HAVE YOU KICKED IN THIS
WEEK? PROBABLY NOT ENOUGH, I CAN TELL YOU
THAT!!!!!

Cheers. YUL *hands the guitar back to* TODD. KLIEG THE BUTCHER
rushes the stage, roaring like a lion, offers his hand.

SADIE Don't fall for it, Yul.

KLIEG THE BUTCHER What, a man can't congratulate his
  neighbor anymore?
SADIE Don't do it, Yul. Trust me, he has the strongest right hand
  in the world.

YUL *accepts the handshake and* KLIEG THE BUTCHER *attempts to
crush* YUL'*s hand, but* YUL *is unfazed and exhibits shocking strength in
his own right hand. Accompanied by a score of drums, this battle goes
on for a few moments and then* KLIEG THE BUTCHER *gives up and
exits very quickly, embarrassed and furious.*

SADIE Wow. Yul, that was . . . *(to Sorrel)* Did you see that?!

SORREL I don't think anyone's actually ever done that before.
  Whenever Klieg the Butcher shakes someone's hand, they
  usually wind up wearing a big white cast for a couple of
  months.
SADIE Yul, are you okay? Is your hand broken? Can you make a fist?
YUL My hand is fine.
SORREL Wow!!! I think I need a cold refreshment!!!

SORREL *exits, amazed, backing out of the room.*

YUL Sadie.
SADIE *(getting herself together)* Yes, Yul? I mean Yul, yes?
YUL Can I have my tooth back now?
SADIE Of course.

*She reaches into her purse, removes a small square of tissue, unwraps it,
considers the tooth for a moment, doesn't yet give it to him.*

SADIE But before I give you your tooth back I'd like to proposition you, and I'm not normally one to be so forward, so I hope this doesn't come off the wrong way.

YUL What.

SADIE Well, what do I have to lose, I guess I'll just say it. *(She gathers her will.)* Will you go home with me? I only live about ten minutes away and it's really a cozy little place and I'd be happy to make you a sandwich.

YUL Sadie, I'm afraid I'm not a very sexual person.

SADIE No, I wasn't . . . Oh, no . . . That didn't exactly come out right, did it?

YUL I could learn stuff, but you might be better off asking someone else. Klieg the Butcher seems pretty sexual.

SADIE Klieg the Butcher! No, no, no! Hmmmm . . . How to put it . . . Maybe I could go home with *you*?! I know it's quite forward of me to ask, Yul, but . . . Please. Just for a little while. I don't want to be alone tonight.

YUL My place isn't very fancy.

SADIE That's okay.

YUL And it's pretty small. I sleep on a cot.

SADIE We don't have to sleep. We can just sit around and listen to the radio.

YUL My clock radio doesn't draw very good reception.

SADIE Then we can have a nice chat. I always love a good chat . . . So I can come over?

YUL I s'pose.

SADIE Great. That's just great. So shall we?

YUL Um . . .

SADIE What is it?

YUL You still have my tooth.

SADIE Oh dear. I'm so sorry.

She hands him his tooth. He looks at it for a moment.

SADIE Is it okay?

YUL It looks like a wolf's.

He puts it in his pocket. They exit.

SCENE 4
Yul's Basement Apartment

Cement walls and a cement floor. A cot. A desk. A chair. A shower stall with a generic shower curtain. A small window high on the cinder-block wall. Bars in front of the window. Water stains on the walls. A trunk at the foot of the cot. A minifridge. A standard phone on the desk as well as a portable double-burner stovetop with a small saucepan. A cheap radio alarm clock. A large hardcover book on the desk as well; the dust jacket is covered with butcher paper. Against one wall, an enormous metal armoire, like a large metal locker. It is locked with a Master Lock. In the center of the room, a large, manhole-like drainage hole with a grille over it. The hole periodically gurgles.

SADIE It's so spartan.

YUL I like to keep things simple.

SADIE Simplicity is an admirable quality . . . *(covering her nose)*
What's that smell?

YUL The sewage plant is about a half a mile down the road.
You'll get used to it in a minute. I have a Millennium CBRN
First Responder gas mask if you'd like to put it on.

SADIE No thanks.

She looks around.

SADIE So much cement. Does it get cold in the winter?

YUL A little. But toward the end of the fall I start using a lot of
Bengay. And I have army blankets.

SADIE Were you in the army?

YUL They wouldn't let me in 'cause of my condition.

SADIE What condition?

YUL I have this thing called myxedema.

SADIE What's that?

YUL It's where my thyroid's in a state of perpetual atrophy.

SADIE But I would think the army would be lucky to have
someone like you. I mean, you have such a strong right hand.

YUL But no one wants a guy with thyroid problems.

SADIE But you went out and got the blankets anyway.

YUL Does that make me a profound loser?

SADIE No, it's just interesting. How does your condition affect you?

YUL It basically makes me feel slow and dumb.

SADIE Do you take medication for it?

YUL I was taking this replacement hormone called thyroxin, but
that just kept making me feel like I was gonna put my head
through this vending machine on the third floor of my former
employer. And then I started punching parking meters, which
didn't make me too popular with the police.

SADIE Have you been arrested or something?

YUL No. But now they follow me around.

SADIE Can't you go back to the doctor and have him change your
medication?

YUL After they fired me I lost my medical benefits. You can sit on
the bed if you want. The bed or the chair. Or the floor, too, but
I wouldn't advise that, as it's had its share of semihazardous
chemicals spilled on it.

She considers all three possibilities, chooses the chair. He sits on the end of the bed. Awkward pause.

SADIE I'm suddenly quite famished. You wouldn't happen to have a piece of fruit lying around, would you? A banana or a tangelo?

YUL I can't keep perishables.

SADIE Why not?

YUL Rats.

SADIE Rats?!

YUL Yeah, they're pretty interested in my life, but they usually only come around when it rains.

SADIE Well, what about your eggs?

YUL I don't consider them food items.

SADIE What do you consider them?

YUL They're more like color-coded containers. But that subject needs to end forever.

Suddenly, the sound of rain. Sadie lifts her feet off the floor, places her heels on the edge of the chair.

SADIE What about chamomile tea, would you happen to have any of that?

YUL No. But I could go get you some. There's a Shell station just down the road. I'm pretty sure they'd have some, as gourmet hot beverages have obviously become our new national pastime.

SADIE No, that's okay. I'll be fine.

She looks around a bit.

SADIE What's in the locker?

YUL A project I'm working on.

SADIE Oh, what kind of project?

YUL I can't really talk about it.

SADIE Are you an artist or something?

YUL There is art involved, but that's all I'm gonna say.

SADIE So mysterious.

She spies the book on his desk.

SADIE What are you reading?

YUL Just this book.

SADIE What's it called?

YUL *Three Hundred and Seventy-five Thousand, Four Hundred and Thirteen Ways to Make a Bomb.* It's pretty informative.

SADIE Oh, I just love to read. I'm currently immersed in a new novel by the author Selden Covington. Have you ever heard of him?

YUL No.

SADIE Well, he's a wonderful writer. His new book is called *Semitones*, and it's about a little girl from Tallahassee, Florida, who has the unusual ability to understand dolphin language. And the government abducts her because it's been revealed that a certain family of dolphins on the Gulf Coast has been communicating with a Middle Eastern terrorist cell called Jolly-Ruk-Funama, and she's the only one who can go "under," as it were, and intercept the essential information.

YUL Dolphins don't talk to terrorists.

SADIE Well, I know that, but it's fiction.

YUL Sounds like miscreantic subterfuge to me.

SADIE I think Selden actually intends the novel to function as a kind of geopolitical satire.

YUL What, you know the guy or something?

SADIE Who, Selden Covington? No, why?

YUL You just called him by his first name. Like you've loved each other next to a roaring fire.

SADIE Well, when he did his author appearance at the mall last year he *did* sign one of his books for me. He was kind enough to shake my hand in a gentlemanly manner, but I would never pretend to actually know him.

YUL I suppose you remember his cologne, too.

SADIE No, I don't. His nostrils were rather hairy, though. That I *do* remember.

YUL I used to know a dog who could say a few things in Spanish.

SADIE How interesting. What could he say?

YUL *"Vámanos a la biblioteca."* And he could say "happy birthday," too, but I can't remember what that is.

SADIE *Feliz cumpleaños.*

YUL What?

SADIE *Feliz cumpleaños.* That's the Spanish phrase for "happy birthday."

YUL Oh, then it was something else. Maybe it was the word for ChapStick.

SADIE I'm afraid I don't know that one . . . When's *your* birthday?

YUL Why, are you involved with some sort of database?

SADIE No. I just like to know when people were born.

YUL That kind of information makes me feel like I have scabs all over my body. Birthdays. Social security numbers. Area code sequences. Any numerical system in which the regulators of the machine can will their logarithmic authority.

Awkward pause. The sound of rain has gotten louder.

SADIE Wow. It's really coming down out there.

YUL Don't worry about the rats. If we keep talking they'll stay away.

SADIE Where do they come in?

YUL Mostly through the drain there. They're pretty good at squeezing through the little holes.

SADIE Can't you plug them?

YUL I can't do that. The drain has to be functional in case of flooding.

SADIE What do you do if the rats get in?

YUL I mostly just start yelling. And if that doesn't work, I do this.

He crosses to his trunk, opens it, removes a toy xylophone, runs the mallet across it and yells—or groans rather—three times, then places it on his desk.

SADIE Do you keep all of your instruments in the trunk?

YUL Only the xylophone. The other ones were destroyed in a fire.

SADIE I'm sorry to hear that.

YUL Yeah, I'm pretty sure it was arson. This rival garage band called The Four-Headed Mexican had it in for me and burnt my garage down while I was in Alaska visiting my uncle Sturgis.

SADIE You have an uncle who lives in Alaska?

YUL Uncle Sturgis is dead now, but he worked on pipelines and did a lot of salmon fishing. When I got home from that one trip the garage was burnt down, and my life has sort of sucked ever since.

SADIE Did you ever press charges against The Four-Headed Mexican?

YUL They changed their name to Wizard Fist and moved to Costa Rica. Plus they were really into disguises, so they pretty much got away with it.

SADIE What happened to your house?

YUL It was attached to the garage.

Pause.

YUL Some of the bigger rats aren't too fazed by the xylophone, but for them I have a special surprise.

SADIE What?

YUL A Taser gun.

SADIE Oh. Is that in your trunk, too?

YUL No. I keep that hidden. It has a shaped pulse discharge of 50,000 units, with a peak voltage of 2.1 milliamps and a striking range of over four and a half meters, so it's highly effective in dispatching anything up to about fourteen pounds. Even large, cartilage-rich rodents.

The drain gurgles.

SADIE Yul, may I use your bathroom?

YUL I don't have a proper latrine on the premises. But you can use the shower. Just make sure to rinse your waste. Especially if you have to make feces.

SADIE Okay.

She takes her purse and exits into the shower stall, drawing the curtain behind her. YUL *opens his minifridge, which is stocked with eggs; he removes a few. He starts the mini-stovetop and then drops the eggs into the saucepan, which is already filled with water. Moments later, the sound of crying can be heard coming from behind the shower curtain.* YUL *listens from the desk. It goes on for a bit and then is replaced by the sound of the shower starting. The phone rings. It rings several times.* YUL *watches the phone as the shower continues to run. The ringing eventually stops. After a brief pause, the phone begins ringing again. As before,* YUL *simply watches the phone. After several rings it ceases. Then the sound of the shower ceases. Moments later,* SADIE *enters from the shower stall. Her hair is wet and she is fully dressed.*

SADIE Hi.

YUL Hello.

SADIE I took a shower. I hope you don't mind.

YUL Was the water colder than death?

SADIE No, it was actually quite warm.

YUL I don't have any proper bath towels, but I keep a roll of Bounty in there.

SADIE I know. I used a few sections.

YUL Did you wash your hair with the Palmolive?

SADIE No.

YUL The only reason I ask is 'cause even though Palmolive is meant for dishes, I use it on my hair, too, because shampoo is an egregious cultural fraud.

SADIE How is shampoo a fraud?

YUL Most shampoos are really just surfactant, industrial detergents with fragrance added. It all drips out of the same vat. Manned by a robot with vitriform eyes and homodont dentistry. The difference is mostly the added fragrance and the packaging.

SADIE I hadn't realized that.

YUL Well, no one in a capitalistic, free-market economy would actually admit that, but it's the truth. It's all about product variance and little white consumer lies.

SADIE I didn't wash my hair, anyway. But the bar of soap was certainly nice.

YUL Yeah, well, that's unscented Lava. I don't have a problem with that particular brand 'cause it tells you exactly what it is. It's not one of those phony luxury soaps . . . You have nice arms, by the way.

SADIE Oh. Thank you.

She tries to cover her arms with her hands.

YUL Can I hold one of them?

She is embarrassed, continues trying to cover them.

YUL If you don't want me to, you can just say it.

SADIE No, I . . . Please.

She offers an arm. He crosses to her, takes it, holds it for a moment.

YUL Has anyone ever painted one of your arms?

SADIE No.

YUL They should.

SADIE Thank you, Yul—I mean, Yul, thank you. That's a very nice thing to say.

He continues holding her arm.

SADIE Yul?

YUL Yes?

SADIE Do you think it could be possible for me to see your
  self-defense suit?

YUL Why, you need a good laugh or something?

SADIE I won't laugh at all. I actually think it's quite
  interesting-looking.

YUL *crosses to his closet, starts to open the door, stops.*

YUL If you laugh I'll have to ask you to leave.

SADIE I promise I won't.

YUL *opens the closet door. Hanging to the left of the dowel are three
outfits identical to the one he is wearing: orange Hawaiian shirts and
three pairs of JCPenney Plain Pockets. To the right is the self-defense
suit.* SADIE *walks up to it, takes it in at a closer proximity, then turns
to him.*

SADIE Will you put it on?

YUL Um . . . Sure. Why?

SADIE I don't know. I just . . . Would you?

*He removes the self-defense suit, considers it briefly, and then crosses to
the shower stall. He pulls the shower curtain aside, exits into the shower
stall, resets the shower curtain.*

SADIE *rises and crosses to the wall locker. She reaches out to touch it. The drain gurgles.* SADIE *retracts her hand, turns to the drain, watches it for a moment, then quickly crosses back to the chair and sits, raising her feet so her heels are on the chair.*

YUL *enters from the shower stall wearing his self-defense suit.* SADIE *stands, mesmerized.*

YUL Do I look like an ass?

SADIE No, not at all. Does it itch?

YUL Sometimes.

SADIE And it really helps protect you from all of those punches?

YUL Pretty much.

SADIE May I touch it?

YUL Hello. I mean, okay.

She rises off the chair, crosses to him, reaches slowly toward his arm. She touches the padding, prodding it a bit. Then she turns away suddenly, quickly crosses back to the chair, sits.

SADIE So I want to tell you something, Yul, and I don't know why I'm telling you because I hardly know you and I haven't shared this with anyone—not even Sorrel Haze, and she's my best friend. By the way, is that okay—that I just used your name in the middle of a sentence?

YUL Middle of the sentence is okay.

SADIE Good. I'm glad . . . *(She gathers her will.)* You see, Yul, I've been having this problem lately where I think something horrible is going to happen to me. It's a little hard to explain, but I feel terrified almost every minute of every day. In bed at night. At the office. While selecting fruit in the produce section at the grocery store.

I live on the top of Hill Street. In a little blue house with white shutters. It's a pretty modest house, but it has a yard and an excellent view of Norvis Woods, and lately I've had this insistent feeling that a beast—a sort of yellow-eyed half-man/half-wolf—is going to come creeping out of the woods intending to harm me. I see him walking upright. With mangy fur and preternaturally human hands instead of paws. For some reason, I can't get him out of my head. Just last night I couldn't fall asleep because every time I closed my eyes I saw him standing over my bed with those hands. His yellow eyes glowing. It was so real I could almost smell his breath.

And it's not only the wolf man; it's other things as well. For instance, last week I was buying stamps at the post office and I almost became paralyzed with the fear that I was going to be abducted. By whom, I don't know. The security guard had to escort me out to my car.

And I don't really know where this all comes from, because nothing's really ever happened to me. I've never had an experience like you had with those kung fu Rollerbladers. I've never been harmed. I'm not a rape survivor. I've never been afraid of the dark. I haven't received any threatening phone calls. I'm generally not even intimidated by the idea of a horror movie. It's just this unmanageable crushing feeling of terror and helplessness.

YUL Welcome to America, enjoy the view of our manifold strip malls and roadside horror outlets.

SADIE What does that mean?

YUL It means that the operators of the machine want you to be afraid so you'll buy more stuff. That's why every media outlet is so oversaturated with violence. They want us all to be good Americans. The directives don't come from a man with a little mustache standing at a podium barking out orders. It's much more subtle than that. Our totalitarian maniac is the invisible radio wave, the pixel on your television screen, the airbrushed cheekbones in the magazine ad. Take any four hours of network television and what do you see? Violent content interspersed with cell phone commercials. And ads for fast food and chocolate bars and beauty products. If I buy that Kit Kat bar maybe I'll feel better. If I eat that Quarter Pounder with cheese then maybe I'll forget that I'm about thirty years away from dealing with my own sedimentary rot. Consumption equals comfort. The more comfortable we are, the less we question. The less we question, the more the machine can continue spinning on its deified industrial sprocket. The anesthetized don't want to know where the needle comes from; they just want to feel good.

SADIE I don't know, though. It's not like I'm hanging out at the mall buying stuff. This feels more personal than that.

YUL Are you afraid of me?

The phone rings. YUL *doesn't move to answer it. They stare at each other. It rings nine or ten times and then ceases.*

SADIE Who keeps calling you?

YUL Probably my former employer.

SADIE Why won't they leave you alone?

YUL Because before I left I urinated on the coffeemaker and

made feces on my boss's desk. I'm sure they'd like to see me rot in jail.

SADIE You should get an answering machine. Then you could screen your calls.

YUL I don't believe in answering machines. Encoded voices. Numerical murmuring. I don't like being reminded that I'm being monitored.

SADIE Monitored by whom?

YUL The overseers of the oligarchy. Also known as the Great Digital Eye.

SADIE Which is part of the machine.

YUL Exactly.

SADIE But what if your mother calls?

YUL My mother doesn't call.

SADIE Why not?

YUL She lives in Tucson, Arizona, with a drone named Blake Van Trapp, and she exists largely on daytime television, chain-store caffeinated beverages, and megacorporate pharmaceuticals.

SADIE What about your dad?

YUL My dad died when I was four.

SADIE How did he die?

YUL He was mauled by wolves.

SADIE Well, that's very sad.

YUL It is what it is.

SADIE My parents passed away just over a year ago. They both died in their sleep. Within three days of each other.

YUL Who went first?

SADIE My mother. My dad couldn't even last seventy-two hours without her.

YUL Sometimes I think people get abducted and their insides get replaced with vacuum-cleaner parts.

SADIE What people?

YUL The people who matter most.

Pause.

SADIE Yul, will you do me a favor?

YUL If you need money, I don't have any.

SADIE I don't need money. I was actually hoping that you could simply tell me something.

YUL What.

SADIE That everything's going to be okay.

YUL Why?

SADIE Because it would mean a great deal to me.

YUL Everything meaning what?

SADIE Everything meaning . . . well, just everything.

YUL Um . . .

SADIE Please, Yul, just say it. And I'd appreciate it if you would incorporate my name. You can even position it at the end of the sentence if you'd like. I don't mind that.

YUL But, what if everything *isn't* going to be okay? That would make me a liar.

SADIE *(a sudden realization)* Oh, this is so embarrassing. I should probably go.

YUL Don't go.

SADIE No, I've taken this too far.

YUL Sadie, please don't go . . . You want me to say it, I'll say it. Everything's gonna be okay, okay?

SADIE You really think so?

YUL Yes.

SADIE Say it again.

YUL Everything's gonna be okay.

SADIE And use my name.

YUL Sadie, everything's gonna be okay.

SADIE I really need that to be true.

Pause.

SADIE Can I stay with you tonight?

YUL Sadie, I already told you I'm not a very sexual person.

SADIE As friends. I won't get in the way, I promise.

YUL Do you snore?

SADIE Yes. Why?

YUL The rats like snoring. I'm pretty sure they think it's a mating call. Nose strips help.

SADIE Nose strips?

He opens his desk drawer, removes a pair of nose strips, peels them off their packaging, puts one on. She does the same.

SADIE Yul, I'm sorry about your misfortunes at the television plant.

YUL Knobs were getting boring, anyway.

SADIE And that's so sad about your dad.

YUL Wolves don't know any better.

SADIE I think your eggs are boiling.

YUL *crosses to the desk, turns the stovetop off. He then puts a pair of yellow rubber gloves on.*

YUL I'm gonna have to ask you to close your eyes for a minute.

She nods, closes her eyes.

YUL Please don't peek.
SADIE I won't.

YUL takes the saucepan and crosses to the large armoire-like locker, sets the saucepan on the top of the locker, removes a key from around his neck, undoes the Master Lock, opens the locker to reveal a meticulous assortment of brightly colored Easter eggs. He reaches into the saucepan, removes four or five eggs, and sets them in a small pan of dye on a shelf in the locker, then closes the locker, relocks it, returns the saucepan to the mini-stovetop, and removes the yellow rubber gloves.

YUL You can open your eyes now.

She opens her eyes.

YUL Take the cot.

She crosses to the cot, gets in with her clothes on.

YUL crosses to the closet. From a shelf, he removes three or four extra-large rattraps. He starts to set them around the room.

YUL Just to be safe.

She nods.

When he is finished setting the traps, he crosses to the closet, starts to take his self-defense suit off.

SADIE Oh, don't take it off.

He stops.

SADIE Just leave it on until I fall asleep.

He crosses back to the desk, sits. The drain hole gurgles.

SADIE Yul, where do you think those kids from Bloggs Junior
   High are?
YUL I don't know.
SADIE It's so strange how people can just disappear like that,
   right?
YUL Sometimes people fall into holes.

YUL *lowers his head, falls fast asleep at the desk.* SADIE *crosses to him at his desk, grabs the mallet to the toy xylophone, plays a simple three-note melody. She plays it twice, watches him sleep as lights fade.*

SCENE 5
Yul's Basement Apartment

YUL *is sleeping at his desk, his head resting on his book, next to the* *xylophone. He is still wearing the self-defense suit and nose strip. He is* *also clutching his Taser gun.* SADIE *is not in the cot. The cot is made* *very neatly. A radio alarm clock sounds.*

RADIO ANNOUNCER VOICE And the total number of missing children from Bloggs Junior High School has now reached an alarming fourteen. The most recent student added to the list is twelve-year-old Andrea Malloy, who never made it home from band practice last night. Area officials have declared it to be the most stunning rash of unexplained disappearances in the history of Norvis County.

YUL *turns the alarm off. He sits up, looks around. The rattraps are still* *set, unsprung. He crosses to the shower stall, pulls aside the curtain,* *crosses to the cot, touches the neatly made surface, sits on the cot.*

End of Act I

ACT II

SCENE 1
The Big Beat-Down Self-Defense Studio/Kiff's Karaoke

YUL *is standing on the encounter mat, wearing his self-defense suit. He is also wearing a large mouth guard now. A buzzer sounds. Moments later,* SADIE *runs on and attacks him. The incantation "Take it back! Take it back! Take it back!" sounds through a bullhorn, with other women's voices accompanying the leader. There is percussive accompaniment from* BOB BEARD, *who is drumming in the back room of Kiff's. After the first sequence,* SADIE *helps* YUL *up off the ground.*

SADIE *(quickly)* I'm sorry I wasn't there when you woke up I thought I heard a rat and there was lots of gurgling in that drain and I had to go home and water my plants.

The second buzzer sounds, cuing the second beat-down. The same incantation, the same teeming women's voices. SADIE *starts to beat* YUL *to percussive accompaniment from* BOB BEARD *in the back room of Kiff's. After she has put* YUL *to the ground, the women cheer.* SADIE *helps* YUL *up off the floor.*

SADIE *(quickly)* Tonight's a big night at Kiff's. Throw-down Thursdays. People go head-to-head—all originals again. My friend Isaak will be there. He's Sorrel Haze's husband. He's a Russian poet and he's really good at karaoke. I think you'll like him. Will you meet me there?

YUL Okay.

SADIE *(quickly)* By the way, what size foot do you have?

YUL Thirteen. Why?

The third buzzer sounds, cuing SADIE*'s final beat-down. The same incantation, the same voices.* SADIE *beats* YUL *to percussive accompaniment from* BOB BEARD, *playing in the back room of Kiff's. After she has beaten* YUL *to the floor, the women in the studio cheer.*

SCENE 2
Kiff's Karaoke

KLIEG THE BUTCHER *is seated at his corner table, brooding over a pitcher of beer.* SADIE, ISAAK GLINKA, *and* SORREL HAZE *are sitting at another table.* YUL *enters.*

SADIE Yul, this is my friend Isaak.
YUL Hello.
ISAAK It is with very much pleasure to meet you.

They shake.

SORREL *(offering her hand)* Yul Carroll.
YUL *(taking her hand)* Sorrel Haze.

They shake.

SORREL Yul blew this joint up the other night. We'll see what
he's got in store for us tonight. I'll be back in a minute. I gotta
go check on the band.

SORREL *exits.*

SADIE Isaak is a poet.
ISAAK I am custodial associate, really.

SADIE During the day he works as a janitor at the junior high school.

YUL Over at Bloggs?

ISAAK Bloggs Junior High, yes.

SADIE Any news on those kids?

ISAAK No news, I'm afraid. It is very sad what has forsaken to those childrens.

SADIE Isaak is from Russia. What's your hometown called?

ISAAK I hail from small village just outside Moscow called Krasnoarmeisk. Famous for its military self-defense systems and pharmaceutical industries.

YUL Sounds just like the heartland.

ISAAK What is heartland?

SADIE The heartland is the central area of a country that has special economic, political, military, or sentimental significance.

ISAAK The midwife of west, no?

SADIE The Midwest, yes.

YUL Amber waves of grain and silos of plutonium.

SADIE Isaak moved here three years ago and fell in love with Sorrel and now they're married.

ISAAK We meet in library while I research magical properties of frog urine. The mythical caxy leaps joyously from lily pad to lily pad, croaking through the misty ponds of time.

SADIE Such lovely imagery, Isaak.

ISAAK Thank you, Sadie. I have many grateful feelings for your kindhearted sentiments. Now I go purchase alcoholic beverages.

SADIE Isaak, Yul doesn't drink alcohol.

YUL I'll take a Shirley Temple.

ISAAK It will be my pleasure to go intercept for my new friend a Shirley Temple.

ISAAC *exits to the bar.* SADIE *and* YUL *are alone.*

SADIE Hi.

YUL Hello.

SADIE Did you enjoy class?

YUL Class was okay.

SADIE I thought you handled the beatings quite effectively. Is it hard to keep getting up off the floor?

YUL It's better than making knobs.

SADIE I've been feeling less afraid today.

YUL That's good.

SADIE Yeah. After class I went home and took a shower without locking the bathroom door. And then I opened the blinds of my kitchen window. Tomorrow I might even take a stroll into the woods.

YUL What about the wolf man?

SADIE Well, he's not really there, right?

ISAAK *returns with drinks.*

ISAAK For the handsome lady, a cosmopolitan. And for Mr. Yul, a refreshing Shirley Temple.

YUL Thanks, Isaak.

SADIE *(to* ISAAK*)* And what are you drinking?

ISAAK I drink sweet nectar from breast of humble cow. Milk with sugar. *Chtob vse byli zdorovy. (He says "cheers" in Russian.)*

They all clink glasses and drink.

SORREL HAZE *takes the stage with* BOB BEARD *and the Unholy Stones, who have already sound-checked by now and are ready to play. She grabs a mic and starts the evening.*

SORREL All right, everyone. Looks like it's about time to get this fuckin' show on the road. Welcome to Throw-down Thursdays! Woooooo!!! Fuck yeah!!! . . . So I'm gonna kick things off tonight with a new song I've been thinking about a lot lately, called "Speak the Truth, Don't Be a Loser." Hit it, Bob Beard!!!

BEARD *starts a percussive punk-rap beat that* TODD *accompanies on the electric guitar.*

SORREL *(singing/rapping)*
  Speak the truth
  Don't be a loser
  Speak the truth
  Don't be so scared
  I've got bullet-hole eyes
  With diamonds inside them
  And a bullet-hole heart
  Where my pain begins

When they call out your number
Say, "That's not my name!"
When they start to encode
Say, "You know not my soul!"
When they ask you a question
Give them four thousand answers
And four thousand pictures
From the fire in the hole

But speak the truth
And don't be a loser
Speak the truth
Don't be so scared
There's a new way of thinking
And adding the numbers
Let the lies kill the rodents
And the truth find the bear

So speak the truth
Uh-huh
Speak the truth
Let it fly now
Speak the truth . . .
Look it up!
Let's spell it! T . . . R . . . U . . . T . . . H!!!

Applause.

SORREL So speak the truth, right? Yeah!!! Fuck yeah!!! So who's
gonna follow that?!

ISAAK *stands.*

SORREL Isaak Glinka. My main flame. Get on up here, lover.

ISAAK *crosses to the stage and* SORREL *kisses him mightily.*

SORREL What are you gonna sing for us tonight, Isaak?

ISAAK When I was young boy living in Krasnoarmeisk, I love the
music of the magic flute. I would sit by pond of black
sparrows and rest my head on mossy stone of tears and let its
melody soothe my misfortunes and wayfaring troubles. Now
in my new country there is no magic flute. But the melody is
still inside me. Like a baby bird chirping in a damp nest. So I
sing for you a song of hope and rejuvenation.

ISAAK *nods to* BOB BEARD *and* TODD *and they begin a Russian folk
fever.*

ISAAK *(singing)*
    Positive identity
    Lumbering in destiny
    Stitched with little majesty
    The small details that God can see

    The dumpling in the chicken broth
    The wheat, the horse, the field, the trough
    Polarity of love and creed
    And caramel to stick to teeth

The red red wine, the pressing hand
The breath of lovers bold and bland
Corn, croissant, carnivore, canned,
Clemency, chlorine, can a man

Know
How it feels to be a woman
Loved by man
Wanting to feel
What woman feels?

Wish I, he can.

ISAAK *ends the song with a flourish. Tremendous applause.* KLIEG THE
BUTCHER *rushes the stage, offers his hand in congratulations. Just as*
ISAAK *is about to execute the handshake,* YUL *storms the stage and taps*
KLIEG THE BUTCHER *on the shoulder.*

YUL Klieg!

KLIEG THE BUTCHER *turns.*

YUL *(offering his hand instead)* I am meat that moves!

YUL's *handshake drives* KLIEG THE BUTCHER *to his knees, breaks his
hand.* KLIEG THE BUTCHER *cries out in pain, gets to his feet, lurches
out of the bar, humiliated.*

SCENE 3

Sadie's Kitchen/Yul's Basement Apartment

SADIE *is pacing back and forth in her kitchen with the phone.*

In YUL's *apartment,* YUL *is at his desk, boiling eggs and reading his book. The phone rings. He lets it ring several times, staring at it. He snatches the phone, answers it.*

YUL THUNDER! FLAMES! ANNIHILATION! AN EXPLOSION YOU HAVE NO CONCEPT OF WILL ROCK YOUR POISONOUS LAIR!!!

SADIE Yul, it's Sadie.

YUL Oh. Sadie. Hello. Sorry, I thought you were someone else.

SADIE It's okay . . . I just wanted to call and tell you how great I thought you were tonight. The way you handled Klieg the Butcher was quite impressive . . . So would you like to have dinner at my house on Friday night? I was thinking of inviting Sorrel and Isaak, too.

YUL Okay.

SADIE Great . . . So what do you like to eat?

YUL Meat mostly.

SADIE Like a roast?

YUL It doesn't matter. As long as it's well done.

SADIE Any sides?

YUL I like corn.

SADIE Anything else?

YUL Hot dogs.

SADIE Hot dogs to start?

YUL Yeah, that sounds good.

SADIE Okay, then. We'll start with hot dogs and move to a roast
with corn. And root beer to drink?

YUL Either that or Hi-C Flashin' Fruit Punch.

SADIE Hi-C Flashin' Fruit Punch! Excellent! So, I'll see you Friday
then.

YUL Okay.

She hangs up.

SADIE *(singing, simply)*
Happy
Happy, happy
Happy, happy, happy . . .

YUL *stares at his eggs boiling.*

SCENE 4

Klieg the Butcher's Butcher Counter

KLIEG THE BUTCHER *is behind his counter, wearing his butcher whites. His apron is splattered with blood. His right hand is in a cast. With his left hand he is chopping meat with a cleaver and listening to death metal, like old Judas Priest, which blares from a boom box on top of the counter. He stops chopping the meat and then grabs a hand strengthener and starts doing left-handed reps.*

SADIE *enters and waits patiently while he finishes his hand-strengthening exercises. He then begins chopping his meat to the music. When he is finished, he stares at her. She points to the boom box. He turns it off, continues staring at her.*

SADIE I'd like to buy some meat.

KLIEG THE BUTCHER What kinda meat?

SADIE Well, perhaps a rump roast.

KLIEG THE BUTCHER What for?

SADIE Well, I'm afraid that's really none of your business.

KLIEG THE BUTCHER Trying to impress your loverboy?

SADIE Maybe I am.

KLIEG THE BUTCHER I wouldn't doubt it if he's had something to do with all of those kids disappearing from the junior high school.

SADIE *(suddenly singing)*

    Run to your mountain
    Run to your mountain
    Run to your mountain
    Run, Klieg, run

    Butcher their hearts
    And blacken the fountain
    Poison the meat
    for everyone.

    Poison the meat!
    Poison the meat!
    Poison the meat!
    Poison the meat!

KLIEG THE BUTCHER Was that supposed to be a song?
SADIE You should be ashamed of yourself!

SADIE *exits.*

SCENE 5

The Bloggs Memorial Library
Checkout Desk

SORREL HAZE *is keying in some information on a computer terminal,*
a stack of books next to her. KLIEG THE BUTCHER *approaches. He is*
wearing a disguise that includes a large mustache and a cowboy hat.
Over his cast he has draped some sort of cloth, like a handkerchief or
perhaps a large oven mitt.

SORREL Can I help you?

KLIEG THE BUTCHER I'd like to register an anonymous tip about
those kids from the junior high.

SORREL Klieg the Butcher, is that you?

KLIEG THE BUTCHER I've never heard of that person in my life.
My name's Vernon Kaywell.

SORREL Oh, how interesting. Well, Mr. Kaywell, the online tip
box is over at the information desk.

KLIEG THE BUTCHER I'd like to just do it here.

SORREL Well, then it's not exactly an anonymous tip. The whole
thing's been set up to protect your anonymity.

KLIEG THE BUTCHER Can't I just write it down on a piece of
paper? I'm not so good with computers.

SORREL *reluctantly produces a small piece of paper and a pen and*
pushes them across the desk to KLIEG THE BUTCHER, *who looks*

around and then begins writing. When he is finished, he folds the piece of paper in half and pushes it back across the table with the pen.

SORREL Mr. Kaywell, your, um, mustache appears to be falling off.

KLIEG THE BUTCHER *quickly corrects it, then turns and exits.*

Moments later, TODD *from Bob Beard and the Unholy Stones approaches the checkout desk. He is also wearing a mustache. It might even be the exact same mustache that* KLIEG THE BUTCHER *was wearing. But he hasn't done a very thorough job of concealing his neon green hair.*

SORREL Can I help you?

TODD Um, I'd like to submit a tip regarding the disappearance of those children from the junior high school.

SORREL Todd?

TODD I'm not Todd. My name's Carlos Lescannick.

She seizes his mustache.

SORREL Oh my fucking god, Todd! Did Klieg the Butcher put you up to this?!

TODD What?

SORREL Did he?!

TODD Sort of.

SORREL Accepting bribes to frame an innocent man? What's wrong with you?

TODD He paid me a hundred bucks! He paid Bob Beard, too! Besides, how do you know he's innocent?!

SORREL In our country a citizen is innocent until proven guilty, Todd. It's one of our basic human rights. It's called the presumption of innocence—maybe you've heard of it? Not that the concept even applies here, because Yul Carroll hasn't been accused of anything! You should be ashamed of yourself!

TODD A hundred bucks is a hundred bucks, Sorrel.

SORREL So what you're saying is that you can pretty much be bought for anything? What's next, Todd, registering local college students to vote Republican?

TODD My name is Carlos Lescannick! And a hundred bucks is more than we make at Kiff's in half a week. *Way* more. And *I* need things, man. I *need* things.

SORREL I'm going to pretend like this never happened, Todd. Get out of my face!

He exits. SORREL is disgusted.

SCENE 6
Sadie's Kitchen/Yul's Basement Apartment

SADIE *is reading* Semitones *at her kitchen table.*

Suddenly a large slab of meat comes crashing through her kitchen window, something a lion would be fed at the zoo.

Terrified, SADIE *slowly crosses to the phone, seizes it, dials.*

In YUL*'s apartment,* YUL *is at his desk, boiling eggs and reading his book. His phone rings. He puts the book down, stares at the phone.*

SADIE Pick up the phone. Please pick up the phone.

YUL *continues staring at the phone. He makes a move to answer it. He hesitates. He then picks it up and hangs up very quickly.*

SADIE *(into the phone)* Yul?

SADIE *stares at the phone in her hand, hangs up, stands very still for a moment, then opens a silverware drawer, removes an enormous knife, and starts to breathe heavily, staring at the knife in her hand.*

A small barbershop. YUL *is seated on a barber throne, wearing a white smock.* CHUCK, *the local barber and owner of the shop, is trimming* YUL's *hair, which is damp and severely parted. In the background, a radio plays old standards.*

CHUCK So what's the occasion, Yul? I only see you a coupla times
   a year.
YUL I have to go to this dinner.
CHUCK Nice. Does this dinner involve a lady?
YUL Sort of, yeah.
CHUCK What's her name?
YUL Sadie.
CHUCK Sadie, huh? Is her last name Hawkins? Just kiddin' . . .

CHUCK *cuts* YUL's *hair, hums along to the music.*

CHUCK So is Sadie pretty?
YUL Yeah.
CHUCK You like her a lot, huh?
YUL She's okay.
CHUCK Yeah, Yul, I'll tell ya. Loneliness'll make a man do some
   interesting things. The year after I got outta barber college, I
   couldn't get a date to save my life. I mean, we all go through
   an awkward stage, right? For whatever reason, women just

didn't find me very interesting. Not that a barber has much to offer—not on paper at least. I stopped shaving. Let my hair grow wild. Started hanging out down by the river. Before I knew it I was talking to unsavory types. The type of men who drink a little more than your standard joes. The type of men who like to get into trouble. I got involved with this one gang of fellas who made it their business to urinate into the gas tanks of police vehicles. "Chuck," they said to me one night, "it's your turn." And you know what I did? I put my willy right there in the opening to the gas tank of a police vehicle and did my duty. Later on we watched the policeman try to start his squad car, and boy, he had some problems. Almost flooded the darn thing—it was hilarious.

My parents wanted me to go into the clergy, but I couldn't convince Father Dempsey that I had the stuff for it. I was headed toward a strange path. Then I met my Ginger at the old midget races over on Farmington Road and everything seemed to get back on track for me. Candlelight dinners. Drive-in movies. The smell of nail polish and Aqua Net. A good woman can change a man. Solve a lotta problems.

He continues trimming YUL'*s hair.*

MALE RADIO ANNOUNCER In area news, the fifteenth student from Bloggs Junior High School has disappeared. Eleven-year-old Corey Blaylock did not come home from school yesterday and law enforcement leaders have declared him to be officially missing as of seven p.m. last night. Local parents are up in arms about the rash of preteen disappearances, and many of them are banding together and refusing to allow their children to go to school, despite the deployment of Bloggs police at the junior high school as well as a task force of undercover officers in the junior high vicinity.

CHUCK It's a real shame about those kids, right? It's hard to believe that there's not one single lead. Sort of a Bermuda Triangle thing.

He continues cutting YUL*'s hair.*

CHUCK You know, one of 'em sat right in this chair about two days before he went missing. This little blond guy named Brady. His mother watched me cut his hair the whole time. She couldn't take her eyes offa him. I gave him a classic flattop with nubbed sides. He wanted little racing stripes over his ears, too, but his mother wouldn't go for it.

When it was over, his mother paid the twelve-fifty and gave him two dollars to tip me with. After he gave me the money, I took his nose. You know, I got your nose, that old routine. I thought it was a nice gesture, but you know what his mother said to me? She said, "Don't do that. He's too old for that." Then she took him by the arm and walked him out.

You know, Yul, I gotta be honest here. A few nights later when I saw his face on the evening news, I cried. I didn't care much for his mother, but I cried for that kid. And you know what else? I didn't sweep up that night, and the following morning when I came in, I separated all of his little blond hairs and put 'em in a plastic bag. I keep it right over there as a sort of vigil, see?

He points to a plastic bag hanging from a hook under a modest crucifix, then continues cutting YUL*'s hair.*

CHUCK Yul, what about you—where do you think they are?

YUL I don't think they're anywhere.

CHUCK What—you think it's all a big hoax?

YUL I think people fall into holes and sometimes the holes close.

CHUCK *nods and continues cutting* YUL*'s hair as the radio plays another standard.*

SCENE 8
Sadie's Kitchen

SADIE, YUL, SORREL, *and* ISAAK *are seated at* SADIE'*s kitchen table, which is fully dressed. They are all eating roast and corn, with a few hot dogs scattered here and there.* YUL'*s hair is combed severely and he is dressed up, which means that he wears a blazer over one of his three orange Hawaiian shirts.*

SORREL Sadie, this roast is incredible. It's so succulent. Isn't it succulent, Isaak?

ISAAK Oh, yes. It practically melts my lips and oral cavity.

YUL Hot dogs are good, too.

SADIE Thanks, Yul. I mean Yul, thanks . . . I'm so glad everyone's pleased with the food.

A pause while people eat.

SORREL So Yul, what's with the new 'do?

YUL I don't know. I thought it was time.

SORREL Well, it looks pretty sharp—how 'bout it, Sadie?

SADIE I think Yul looks very handsome.

Awkward pause. Some eating.

SADIE So Sorrel, how are things at the library?

SORREL Oh, don't get me started.

SADIE What's wrong?

SORREL Well, ever since those children at the junior high school started disappearing, there's been a small but persistent faction of librarians who are trying to have a group of young adult novels taken off the shelf.

SADIE What young adult novels?

SORREL Well, the list has reached upwards of two hundred titles. It's basically any young adult novel that deals with violence or incorporates quote unquote "the trappings of a violent world" as one of its major themes. It's really disgusting. Censorship at your local library. Watch out, America, the sky is indeed falling. And it's definitely blue.

SADIE That's so creepy.

SORREL The ringleader is this sixty-year-old Ernest Borgnine lookalike named Dolores Dean. She's been circulating irate, all-caps memorandums and bum-rushing library members to sign banning petitions. It's like McCarthyism all over again. I mean, it's 2007, right? Who would've thought that books like *Slaughterhouse-Five* and *The Chocolate War* would be facing banning petitions?

SADIE She's trying to ban Vonnegut?

SORREL Vonnegut, Cormier, Brock Cole, M. T. Anderson.

SADIE But M. T. Anderson's a genius! *Burger Wuss* is one of my all-time favorite YAs, not to mention *Feed*!

SORREL *Feed* was at the top of the list. *Feed, Slaughterhouse-Five, The Chocolate War, The Goats.* I walked into the young adult section this morning and there was suddenly so much shelf space, I thought I was at the supermarket during a blowout sale. It's really disgusting. Old crotchety Dolores using the disappearance of those kids as fodder to deploy some

right-wing agenda that she's no doubt been harboring for the
past fifty years.

ISAAK She is most unhappy woman.

SORREL Woman? I doubt the bag of hammers even has a vagina.
If you pulled her pants down you'd probably find a first edition
of *Mein Kampf*.

YUL I read that book. That guy really struggled.

Awkward pause.

SADIE Well, has there been an adverse reaction to Dolores's plot?

SORREL Yeah, there's a handful of us still fighting the good fight,
but we're viewed as being the young dykey punks who the
library board is suspicious of anyway.
  I personally think it's condescending to spare kids from
literature that contains violent content.

SADIE What do you think, Yul?

YUL I think books are more dangerous than anything.

SADIE Why?

YUL Because they get at your thoughts in the most personal way.
The author's voice is like a whisper that finds you at midnight.

SORREL Are you a reader?

YUL Yes.

SORREL Fiction or nonfiction?

SADIE He reads manuals mostly.

SORREL What are you reading now?

SADIE It's called *Three Hundred and Seventy-five Thousand, Four
Hundred and Thirteen Ways to Make a Bomb*.

YUL Take, for instance, that book. If I'm reading about how
nitroglycerin is created by adding glycerol to a mixture of

concentrated nitric and sulfuric acids and how it has a sweet, burning taste, and how when combined with an inert, porous substance such as charcoal or diatomaceous earth it can form a potent and reliable blasting gelatin, then I don't need a bunch of visuals or a multicolored pie chart or some sort of Hollywood-style video presentation, because the words are absorbed so deep in my consciousness that I can see the colorless, semitoxic, somewhat oily liquid standing in a sixteen-inch, hydraulically cooled carbon cylinder.

ISAAK Yul, your way with language is a stunning manifestation of terrible beauty and the most cherished animation of the various catastrophes of passion.

YUL Thanks, Isaak.

ISAAK Yes. I would now like to recite instantaneous poem.

The Herculean stillness
Of great red-tailed hawk
Is not the profound torpor
Of a bird pinned to the heliotrope sky
But rather, it is like patience
Of a wind-softened man
Floating on velvet water.
Behold, fair hawk,
Your flight beckons crystal
From the Sea of Galilee.

SORREL Oh, Isaak, I love it when you talk dirty like that.

SORREL *kisses* ISAAK *full on the mouth.*

SADIE *stares at* YUL, *who meets her gaze for a moment and then looks down at his lap.*

SADIE Shall we have dessert?! There's chilled fruit cups. And pie!

SORREL Oh, Sadie, I think Isaak and I better get home. He has to get up early tomorrow and buff the gymnasium floor.

SADIE Oh, darn!

SORREL *winks at* SADIE *and gestures in such a way as to suggest that she wants to let her friend have some romantic privacy.*

ISAAK The floor buffer is truly masterful device. It reminds me of dancing with my grandma Glinka in great horse stables of old country.

Suddenly, the faraway sound of a wolf howling.

SADIE Oh, no.

SORREL What?

SADIE Didn't you hear that?

SORREL Hear what?

SADIE That howl.

SORREL I didn't hear anything . . . What kind of howl?

SADIE A wolf howl. You sure you didn't hear it?

SORREL Pretty sure, Sadie.

The wolf howl again.

SADIE There it is again! Listen!

They listen.

SORREL I don't hear anything. Isaak, do you hear anything?

ISAAK *Nyet.*

SADIE Yul?

YUL *shakes his head.*

SADIE I can't believe none of you heard that!

SORREL Maybe it's your own little special wolf.

SADIE Why would you say that?

SORREL What?

SADIE I can't believe you would make fun of me in my own kitchen!

SORREL Sadie, calm down. I was joking.

SADIE Well, I don't think it's a joking matter!

An awkward pause.

SORREL Well, on that note . . .

She and ISAAK *rise.*

SORREL Thank you for a lovely dinner, Sadie.

ISAAK It was most crushing and dominant feast.

SORREL Maybe we'll see you guys at Kiff's on Wednesday? The Wal-Mart is donating a George Foreman Lean Mean Fat Reducing Grilling Machine for the lucky winner. You think you'll come by, Yul?

YUL Sure. I'll come.

SORREL Rock on. Well, you two have a good night. *(to* YUL*)*
    Keep that wolf away from my girl.

ISAAK *and* SORREL *exit.*

SADIE *turns and faces* YUL. *She sits. He follows suit. They sit in silence*
for a moment.

SADIE You really didn't hear the wolf?
YUL I didn't hear it.

Awkward pause.

SADIE Would you care for dessert?
YUL I'm pretty full.
SADIE Coffee?
YUL No, thanks.
SADIE Then may I show you something? I'll be right back.

SADIE *exits.* YUL *crosses to the window, touches the paper plate.*

Moments later SADIE *returns wearing a large sponge self-defense suit,*
very similar in make and color to YUL*'s.*

SADIE I ordered it from the catalog at the studio. It's a nice one,
    right?
YUL Yeah. It's way better than mine.
SADIE It has an extra layer of padding in the sternum area. I
    slept in it last night. It was the best night's sleep I've had in a
    long time.

Awkward pause.

SADIE So Yul, will you do me a favor?

YUL What.

SADIE Hit me? Just a few quick combinations. I bought headgear, too, see?

From behind her back she produces padded headgear, puts it on.

YUL Sadie, I don't think I can hit you.

SADIE Oh, please, Yul?—I mean, Yul, oh, please?

YUL I'm sorry, but that's just weird.

SADIE Then can I have a hug?

YUL What do you want from me?

SADIE *(indignant)* What?

YUL One minute you ask me to hit you, the next minute you ask for a hug.

SADIE It must be confusing, I know.

YUL Yeah, people think *I'm* weird.

SADIE I care about you.

YUL Oh, no.

SADIE Yul, I do. More than you know . . . I had a dream about you last night.

YUL Did it involve me falling thousands of feet backwards into a pit of broken glass?

SADIE No, it actually involved you and me on a porch swing. And before us was a big field of corn with a high moon shining down. And there were fireflies and the sound of crickets. The moonlight was making the corn look blue. And we were just sitting there, rocking the swing back and forth with our feet.

And then . . . well, let's just say something very beautiful
happened.

YUL   What, like an animated horse came out of the cornfield
representing the Disney corporation?

SADIE   No, it didn't involve an animated horse. What happened
was very warm and special. In terms of dream interpretation I
think it's pretty obvious . . . I realized after I woke up that I
haven't felt quite the same since the day I knocked your tooth
out. Please sit.

He sits.

She gathers her will.

SADIE   *(suddenly singing)*
  I love you, Yul
  I love you, Yul—
  I mean, Yul, I love you.
  I love you, I do
  I love you, it's true

  There's a bird in my heart
  And it's flying for you
  A sparrow, a little sparrow
  Over fields filled with dew

  I love you, Yul
  I love you, Yul
  I love you . . .

YUL *grimaces epically.*

SADIE Oh, please don't grimace!

YUL Love is an erroneous myth created by the Hallmark corporation.

SADIE The concept of love was around way before the Hallmark corporation!

YUL Then it was created by oppressed medieval serfs to get them through the night.

SADIE What's wrong with needing something to get you through the night?

YUL In my opinion love ranks right up there with Rumpelstiltskin and flying green dragons.

SADIE Yul, don't you feel *anything?*

YUL I feel an ache.

SADIE But don't you understand that I do, too?

YUL My ache has nothing to do with things romantic.

SADIE What does it have to do with?

YUL I don't know. Parking meters. Our system of currency. The concept of one-size-fits-all. I'm gonna go now.

SADIE Yul, please don't go.

She moves to touch him.

YUL Don't!

She stops.

SADIE But I love you. And, who knows, maybe you love me, too, and you just don't know it? You should give it a chance.

YUL I'm leaving now.

SADIE I can't believe you're going to abandon me with that thing out there in the woods. Especially after everything I just told you.

He exits the kitchen. Moments later, the front door closes.

SADIE *stands very stiff, still wearing the suit of sponge, stunned, confused. She starts to hyperventilate. She sits. She cries.*

SCENE 9

Chuck's Barbershop

CHUCK *the barber is sweeping up hair, whistling to an old standard playing on the radio.*

BOB BEARD *from Bob Beard and the Unholy Stones enters. He is in disguise, perhaps wearing a strange hat and funny glasses. He is carrying a paperboy bag and wearing a yellow "community" ribbon.*

CHUCK Can I help you?

BOB BEARD *reaches into his paperboy bag and removes a rolled-up poster, hands it to* CHUCK. *He also hands him a yellow "community" ribbon.*

BOB BEARD It's for the community.
CHUCK Oh. Why, thank you.

BOB BEARD *turns, exits the barbershop.* CHUCK *removes the rubber band, unrolls the poster. It's a large, crude duplicated photograph of* YUL *with devil horns and "STOP HIM!" printed in big block letters across the bottom.* CHUCK *considers the poster for a moment, and looks at the ribbon.*

SCENE 10

Yul's Basement Apartment

YUL *is seated at his desk. Before him is an enormous assortment of dyed
hard-boiled eggs. They are carefully arranged in several egg cartons.
With a large hypodermic needle, he is injecting a mysterious clear liquid
into the crown of one of the eggs. He works meticulously, concentrating
very hard. He stops, looks to his trunk, opens it, removes the toy
xylophone, plays the same three notes that Sadie had played at the end of
Act I. He plays it a few times and then sings with surprising,
heartbreaking power.*

YUL *(singing)*
 SADIE!
 I'M JUST A MAN!
 AND I'M VERY CONFUSED.

A knock on the door.

YUL Who is it?
VOICE UPS.

YUL *places the hypo in the desk drawer, crosses to the door, opens it. A
man in a brown UPS suit is there, holding a brown cardboard box. Like*
YUL, *he speaks in a low-energy, deliberate fashion.*

UPS MAN Yul Carroll?

YUL Yeah, that's me.

UPS MAN Sign here, please.

While YUL *takes the small digital signature board, the* UPS MAN *looks around the room.*

UPS MAN *(referring to the eggs)* Easter's comin' early this year, huh?

YUL I like to get a head start.

UPS MAN Hey, you're that guy on all the posters.

YUL What posters?

UPS MAN The ones with "Stop Him" on them. I just saw one over at the bowling alley. There were like twelve people looking at it.

YUL Huh. Do I look weird on it?

UPS MAN Well, you obviously don't have devil horns in real life. But no, on the poster you actually look pretty much like you do now . . . Whatever you're doing, you're certainly makin' a name for yourself. Keep up the good work.

The UPS MAN *nods a farewell, exits.* YUL *closes the door, takes the package, sets it on the floor, considers it for a moment, and then opens it. Inside is a pair of gray Silver Streak roller skates. He removes the skates, studies them a moment, and then removes his shoes and puts them on. He begins skating around his apartment, slowly at first, and then faster and faster. He enjoys himself. He might even smile. Moments later, another knock on the door.* YUL *stops skating.*

YUL Who is it?

No answer.

He carefully glides to the front door, places his ear to the door, listens.
After a moment, he opens the door and discovers a large slab of raw
meat—enough to feed a lion. YUL looks down the hall, brings the meat
inside, closes and locks the door. There is a note attached to the slab of
raw meat. YUL removes the note.

YUL *(reading the note)* Hey, freak. Meet me in Norvis Woods for a
battle to the death. Midnight tomorrow night. Klieg the
Butcher.

The phone rings. YUL stares at the phone. It rings several times, ceases.
YUL stares at the meat in his hand.

SCENE 11
Kiff's Karaoke

SORREL *and* ISAAK *are consoling* SADIE, *who is terribly upset. On the table is a George Foreman Grill, still in the box. They are all drinking.*

SADIE It was so horrible, you guys. I told him I loved him and he was disgusted.

SORREL I doubt he was disgusted, Sadie.

SADIE Sorrel, he grimaced! People generally grimace when they're sickened by something. For instance, I often grimace when I watch that intestinal surgery show on cable access. Or when I come across a neighbor's cat frozen to the side of a tree in the middle of January. It's such a disaster. Just a few days ago he held my arm and told me it should be painted.

SORREL Sadie, you have to admit, the guy's a little strange. Don't get me wrong, I like him. And Isaak thinks the world of him.

ISAAK I think he is very special person with heart of lemon. I mean lion.

SADIE And he has such a gift for music.

ISAAK I understand he is rock-and-roll sensation.

SORREL That's all very true, but you have to admit, it is possible that there might be a screw loose somewhere. I mean, the guy's read *Mein Kampf* and exhibited sympathy for Hitler.

SADIE He said that the guy *really struggled.*

SORREL But isn't that a little weird?

SADIE I think that's what's so special about him. He can

empathize with even the most horrible social criminal in the history of the modern world.

SORREL No, you're right. You probably just scared him. I mean, you said the guy doesn't even have bath towels. And he lives in that weird basement apartment near the sewage plant.

SADIE He's had a rough life, he really has. His father was mauled by wolves and he was recently attacked by a gang of kung fu Rollerbladers with nunchakus. He obviously has trust issues. Not to mention his thyroid affliction . . . And his rat problem . . . And his difficulty acquiring gainful employment . . .

SORREL Drink, Sadie.

ISAAK Yes, Sadie. We drink and then we cry. And then we turn our lives into beautiful poems to be carved into sides of trees and buildings.

KLIEG THE BUTCHER *enters with a rolled-up poster. His right hand is in a cast. He is wearing a yellow "community" ribbon.*

SORREL Well, if it isn't Klieg the Butcher. Or is that Vernon Kaywell?

SADIE What are you doing here?

KLIEG THE BUTCHER I came to win the George Foreman Lean Mean Fat Reducing Grilling Machine.

SORREL Show's canceled tonight.

KLIEG THE BUTCHER Canceled! Why!?

SORREL Too many assholes on the bill.

KLIEG THE BUTCHER Then I'm just gonna put this poster up. The manager said it was okay.

SORREL It's not my bar.

Somewhere on the stage, prominently placed, perhaps over the drum kit,
KLIEG THE BUTCHER *puts up the poster with the picture of* YUL
CARROLL *that says "STOP HIM!" underneath.*

KLIEG THE BUTCHER *(announcing to the world)* He will be
stopped at all costs!!!

He exits intensely. They stare at the poster.

SCENE 12

Chuck's Barbershop

CHUCK *is in the barber throne, reading the newspaper and listening to an old standard on the radio. He is now wearing a yellow "community" ribbon. He sings along for a moment and then the news comes on.*

RADIO ANNOUNCER In local news, the sixteenth student from Bloggs Junior High School has disappeared. Eleven-year-old Derrick Downs never showed up to his after-school Eagle Scout meeting and has been reported as officially missing as of five-thirty this evening. Police still have no explanation for the mysterious disappearances of all sixteen children, and the Federal Bureau of Investigation has been working with local authorities to compile a list of possible suspects.

In other news, the seventh annual St. Rose of Lima Church Bazaar is scheduled to kick off following this Sunday's morning service. All those interested in attending should be advised that due to construction the church parking lot will be unavailable, and you are encouraged to use the lot at the nearby fairgrounds . . .

YUL *enters. He looks disheveled, windblown, exhausted.*

CHUCK Yul.

YUL Hello, Chuck.

CHUCK You don't look so good.

YUL Who put that poster on your door?

CHUCK Um, actually I did.

YUL Why?

CHUCK This guy came in the other day with posters. It seemed like he was representing a pretty serious concern for the community. I felt it was my civic duty.

YUL I thought you were my friend.

No response.

YUL Do you think I did something to those kids?

CHUCK To be honest, Yul, I don't know. A lot of people are talking. Your name's coming up quite a bit.

Awkward pause. Only the radio.

CHUCK Can I help you with anything else?

YUL I was actually wondering if you would cut my hair again.

CHUCK You're not happy with my work?

YUL No, your work was fine. I'd like it to go away. I was hoping you could shave it off.

CHUCK Yul, I'm afraid I can't help you there. You can get a set of Gold Dollar 9910 clippers over at Kmart for twenty-five ninety-five.

YUL What, you don't want to be known as the barber who shaved the freak's head?

No response.

YUL You never know, Chuck, maybe it would work to your advantage. You could put my hair in a plastic bag and hang it over there on the wall next to the other one. It could be like Hitler's mustache or Ted Bundy's kidney stones or something. I'm sure it would be a good story to tell all your customers.

CHUCK Go home, Yul.

YUL *looks at* CHUCK *for a moment, shakes his head, exits.* CHUCK *watches him leave.*

SCENE 13
The Big Beat-Down
Self-Defense Studio

The incantation of "Take it back! Take it back! Take it back! Take it back!" is fevered and horrible. SADIE *is standing on the encounter mat, wearing her new self-defense suit. She has replaced* YUL *as the "meat man" and is ready to take on a beating from a fellow student. From out of nowhere,* YUL *enters.*

SADIE Yul.

YUL Hello. Tonight I'm gonna meet Klieg the Butcher in Norvis Woods for a battle to the death. My life has suddenly lost all meaning and I just wanted to say good-bye in case you never see me again.

He turns to exit.

SADIE Yul!

He stops, turns back.

SADIE Did you get the skates?

YUL It's the nicest thing anyone's ever done for me. I sleep with them under my pillow. Which sorta hurts, but pain is of little consequence anymore.

SADIE What time are you meeting Klieg the Butcher?

YUL Midnight. But please don't tell anyone.

SADIE I won't.

He turns to exit.

SADIE Yul!

YUL *turns back again.*

SADIE Good luck.

YUL *nods, exits.* SADIE *stares out, stunned, as the incantation "Take it back! Take it back! Take it back!" resumes and she prepares to be assaulted.*

SCENE 14
Norvis Woods/Kiff's Karaoke

Midnight. A clearing in Norvis Woods, surrounded by trees. Moonlight. Fog. Shadows creeping. The sounds of nocturnal birds. YUL *is standing in the middle of the clearing, turning a slow circle, looking around.*

KLIEG THE BUTCHER *emerges from the shadows. He is holding a large butcher knife.*

KLIEG THE BUTCHER Hey, freak.

YUL Hello.

KLIEG THE BUTCHER You ready to die?

YUL Not especially.

They begin fighting. There is accompanying percussion from BOB BEARD, *who is sitting at his kit in the back room of Kiff's Karaoke, where* TODD *is putting up more posters.* KLIEG THE BUTCHER *swipes at* YUL *with the butcher knife.* YUL *jumps back.* KLIEG THE BUTCHER *tries again.* YUL *jumps back. And again.* YUL *grabs his arm. They grapple.* YUL *squeezes* KLIEG THE BUTCHER's *wrist.* KLIEG THE BUTCHER *drops the butcher knife, swipes at* YUL *with his cast, misses.* YUL *throws the butcher knife into the trees.* BOB BEARD *continues scoring the battle on his drum kit.*

From some hidden fold, KLIEG THE BUTCHER produces another butcher knife. He swipes at YUL and misses. He swipes again, misses, but YUL falls trying to get out of the way.

SADIE appears in the clearing. She is frenzied, out of breath. Just as KLIEG THE BUTCHER is about to finish YUL off, SADIE jumps in front of YUL and KLIEG THE BUTCHER strikes her cleanly in the stomach. He drops the butcher knife, shocked.

YUL rises off the ground, clutches KLIEG THE BUTCHER by the throat, squeezes. KLIEG THE BUTCHER gasps for air, begs for his life.

After a moment, YUL releases KLIEG THE BUTCHER. KLIEG THE BUTCHER runs off through the woods.

YUL gathers SADIE in his arms, carries her out of the woods.

The sound of thunderous drums.

SCENE 15
An ICU Room at Bloggs
Memorial Hospital

SADIE *is lying in a hospital bed. Her abdomen is heavily bandaged. On her side table is a copy of* Semitones. *There is an IV fed into one of her arms. She is sleeping.* YUL *is seated beside her in a chair, holding her hand. A* MALE NURSE *enters, checks something on her chart, exits.*

After a moment, SADIE *wakes.* YUL *takes his hand back. She is weak, can't speak so well.*

YUL Hello.
SADIE Hello.

Awkward pause.

SADIE You can keep holding my hand if you want.

He takes her hand.

YUL They found Klieg the Butcher on a Greyhound heading to
    New York City. When the bus got halfway through
    Pennsylvania, he apparently flipped out and tried to take the
    whole bus hostage with a paring knife. So you won't have to
    worry about him for a while.
SADIE I should've worn my suit.

YUL Yeah, I was just thinking that.

He reaches into his pocket, removes a small white handkerchief folded in a square.

YUL I made something for you.

He hands her the handkerchief. She opens it. It is a necklace of his tooth.

YUL It's my tooth.
SADIE I love it.

She puts it on, examines the tooth. A pause.

SADIE Yul, about the other night. I'm really sorry. I said a lot of things that probably sounded really irrational.
YUL It's okay, Sadie. I like you, too.
SADIE You do?
YUL Yeah, I do.
SADIE A lot or a little?
YUL A lot.
SADIE You know, you just used my name at the end of a sentence.
YUL I did?
SADIE Yeah. You said, "It's okay, Sadie." Does that mean you're going to begin the termination process?
YUL No.

Pause. She kisses his hand. They stay that way for a long moment and then YUL *takes his hand back. He stands.*

YUL Well, I should prolly go. The doctor said you need your rest and you shouldn't be talking too much.

SADIE Will you come see me tomorrow?

YUL I don't know. I got something I gotta do. It's pretty important.

SADIE Maybe you could put it off for a while.

YUL Well, I was gonna originally wait till Easter.

SADIE Oh, wait till Easter!

YUL I don't think I can.

SADIE At least think about it.

YUL Okay.

Pause.

SADIE Yul, thanks for the necklace.

YUL *exits.*

SCENE 16

The Hospital Room/Yul's Basement Apartment, Later

SADIE *is lying in bed, reading* Semitones.

In YUL*'s apartment, the sound of the shower running. The wall locker is open and all the eggs are gone.*

In SADIE*'s hospital room, the sound of a wolf howl.*

SADIE *looks around, concerned.*

Another wolf howl.

SADIE *starts to panic, hits the call button several times.*

Moments later, the MALE NURSE *enters.*

MALE NURSE Do you need something?
SADIE Did you hear that howling?
MALE NURSE Howling?
SADIE Yes, howling. Just a few moments ago there were two
    distinct howls and they were quite wolflike.
MALE NURSE I'm afraid I didn't hear them.
SADIE And you were on the floor?

MALE NURSE I've been on the floor all night. My station is just
  outside your door.

SADIE Huh.

MALE NURSE Did you need anything else?

SADIE No thanks.

MALE NURSE Well, just hit the call button if you do. Like I said,
  I'm right outside your door.

She nods. He exits.

Moments later, the wolf howls again. SADIE *panics, tries to sit up, but is
in too much pain.*

The bathroom door opens and an odd WOLF MAN *steps into her
hospital room. He has human hands and stands upright but has the face
of a wolf. He simply stands there, staring at* SADIE.

SADIE *screams and begins desperately hitting the call button.*

The WOLF MAN *turns and goes back into the bathroom, closing the
door behind him.*

Moments later, the MALE NURSE *rushes in.*

SADIE It's in the bathroom!!! Hurry, it's in the bathroom!!!

The MALE NURSE *rushes into the bathroom.* SADIE *is hyperventilating,
terrified. Moments later, the* MALE NURSE *enters from the bathroom.*

MALE NURSE There's nothing in there.

SADIE Oh. Are you sure?

MALE NURSE I'm positive.

SADIE Well, maybe he jumped out the window.

MALE NURSE There's no window.

SADIE Oh.

MALE NURSE Would you like a sedative, Ms. Day?

SADIE No. No thanks.

MALE NURSE Are you sure?

SADIE I don't like people who play tricks with trademark anesthetics.

MALE NURSE No one's playing tricks. And it's not an anesthetic; it's a sedative. It'll just help you relax a little.

SADIE I don't want a sedative.

MALE NURSE What about the TV? Would you like to watch some TV?

SADIE No TV. Maybe the radio.

MALE NURSE No problem.

He crosses to the radio, turns it on to an easy listening station. He then crosses to her IV bag, checks it.

MALE NURSE I'll be right outside, okay?

She nods. He exits.

The radio plays for a moment, perhaps "You Light Up My Life" by Debby Boone. When the song ends, a newscaster takes over.

NEWSCASTER In local news, today's top story was the discovery of sixteen area junior high school students who were found in a bomb shelter under the Bloggs Junior High School gymnasium floor. They were discovered by Isaak Glinka, one of the custodians on staff, who heard what he described as the faraway voices of children while he was buffing the gymnasium floor. (ISAAK) "I buff the floor and I hear voices of childrens and I think I am crazy person. I follow noise to trapdoor under basketball performance floor. I climb down ladder into dark tunnel and follow tunnel many meters. The voices grow stronger and stronger until I come to steel door. When I open door, there they are. It is like miracle."

The bomb shelter, which was built in the late 1940s, had apparently been forgotten about by the current Bloggs Junior High School administration. The sixteen children had been planning the disappearance for some time and had been stockpiling food and water for months. When one of the children was asked *why* they went into hiding, he simply said, "Because we're scared." Mr. Glinka said that when he discovered the children they were linked hand in hand in a candlelit prayer vigil. When asked what they were praying for, Mr. Glinka said that they were simply praying to a Christian God.

In YUL*'s apartment,* YUL *emerges out of the shower. He is naked and drying himself with a roll of paper towels. His and* SADIE*'s radios are tuned to the same station.* YUL *crosses to his closet, opens it, removes the self-defense suit, puts it on.*

NEWSCASTER This just in. Not twenty minutes ago, the Zenith television plant on Old Mill Road went up in flames after an explosion almost rocked the landmark building off its foundation. WXUQ's Dennis O'Shea is live at the Zenith plant. Dennis?

DENNIS O'SHEA *(frantic, the sounds of sirens in the background)*
"Donny, as you can hear in the background, it's mayhem here
at the Zenith plant, with police and firefighters simply trying
to make sense of the melee. The number of deceased and
casualties is unknown at this point as firefighters are simply
trying to get the flames under control.

"Moments ago, Lieutenant Casey Studds told me that he
believes there was arson involved, as the smell produced by the
incineration is common to explosions caused by large amounts
of combustible nitroglycerin. It's truly a harrowing situation
down here at the Zenith plant, one that the city of Bloggs has
never seen before. And it certainly has to make you wonder
what on earth is happening to our country . . ."

After YUL *gets into his self-defense suit, he crosses to his cot, reaches under
his pillow, grabs his roller skates, slings them over his shoulder. He then
crosses to the drain hole in the center of his apartment, removes the
grating, starts to climb down into the hole. When he has fully descended,
he reaches up and pulls the drain grating over him, sealing the hole.*

*On the radio, the announcer continues to report the events surrounding
the explosion at the Zenith plant.*

In the hospital room, SADIE *pulls the covers up to her chin.*

Moments later, in YUL's *apartment, the phone rings several times.*

Blackout.